TABLE OF CONTENTS

INTRODUCTION

This book has been designed to be a simple, clear and thorough tool for the traveler to Spain or Latin America.

Here you will find hundreds of simple expressions that cover the everyday situations you are likely to encounter. You will also find a glossary that puts thousands of words and their pronunciations at your fingertips. The pronunciation system has been designed for simplicity and ease of use. Pronunciation of more difficult words will also be found among the phrases themselves.

Unlike our own language, Spanish is highly regular: Each letter or combination of letters is always pronounced the same way. This makes the pronunciation delightfully simple. It is well worth learning, for once learned, you will be able to pronounce every Spanish word correctly.

Throughout the book there are language and travel tips that you will find valuable. There is also a simple-to-use basic grammar section, a pronunciation key, and several helpful charts.

It is hoped that this book will keep you from letting an unfamiliar language prevent you from experiencing the Latin cultures as joyfully and fully as you otherwise might. Remember, however new you are to the language, your willingness to communicate in it will be appreciated by your hosts and will increase your own pleasure.

GUIDE TO SPANISH PRONUNCIATION

a — as in father

b — as in rainbow, but softer. The lips hardly meet.

c — before e and i, as in cent.* otherwise, as in can

ch — as in choose

d — like th in the

e — like the a in gate; sometimes shortened, almost like the e in cell

f — as in fish

g — before e and i, like an h, strongly aspirated, otherwise, as in go

h — always silent in Spanish

i — like ee

j — like h in hot, strongly aspirated

k — as in key

l — as in lamp

ll — like y in yawn

m — as in man

n — as in nut

ñ — like ni in onion

o — as in hop

p — as in whisper

q(u) — like the k in basket

r — similar to the tt in kitty, pronounced rapidly

rr — like the r, but more strongly trilled

s — as in sell

t — as in tie

u — like the oo in soon

v — see b; these sounds are interchangeable in Spanish

w — as in wax (found only in foreign words)

x — like x in axle; sometimes like an s, or a strongly aspirated h

y — the conjunction y is prounced like ee; otherwise, as in yawn

z — like s in sin*

---

*In Castilian Spanish, pronounced like the th in thin.

Diphthongs

ai
ay } — like the i in wife

au
aoo } — like the ow in cow

ei
ey } — like the a in rate

ia — like ya in yacht
ie — like ye in yet
io — like yo in yogurt
ua — like wa in water
ue — like wa in wait
ui — like wee in week
uo — like uo in quota

Triphthongs

iai — like yi in yipe
iei — like a cheer: yay!
uai — like wi in wine
uei — like wa in wait

Some Notes

In this book:

ā is pronounced like the a in rate;
sometimes in speaking Spanish, the a is shortened to
almost a short e sound, as in men.
For example:

démelo
luego

ay is pronounced like the i in wife
aoo is pronounced like the ow in cow

Remember that although the words given in the Glossary are
common words, there are often other common words for
the same things. Space prohibits listing them all.

Remember that many adjectives have a feminine and a masculine form; because of space limitations, only the masculine form is given.

4

GREETINGS & USEFUL EXPRESSIONS

Good morning. — Buenos días.
Good afternoon. — Buenas tardes.
Good evening. — Buenas tardes.
Good night. — Buenas noches.
Goodbye. — Adiós.
See you later. — Hasta luego. (lwā'-go)
How are you? — ¿Cómo está usted?
(I am) Well, thank you. — Bien, gracias.

Buenos días but
Buenas tardes and
Buenas noches.
Notice the difference!

The "usted" (you) in questions is often understood, and is
sometimes not expressed.
"¿Cómo está?" (How are you?)

The definition and pronunciation of *all* words used will be
found in the Glossary.

Pleased to meet you. — Mucho gusto.
I don't speak Spanish. — No hablo español. (ās-pan-yol')
I speak it a little. — Lo hablo un poco.
How's it going? — ¿Cómo le va?
Excuse me. — Perdóneme. (pār-don'-ā-ma)
Excuse me. (to get past someone) — Con permiso.
Thank you. — Gracias.
You're welcome. — De nada.
What is your name? — ¿Cómo se llama usted? (ya'-ma)
My name is . . . — Me llamo . . .
I don't know. — No sé.

"¿Mande?" is an expression frequently heard in conversa-
tion. It means "What? Please repeat."

I didn't know. — No sabía.

I don't understand. — No entiendo. (ān-tyān'-do)

Do you know him? — ¿Lo conoce usted? (ko-no'-sā)

Do you know her? — ¿La conoce usted?

Where do you live? — ¿Dónde vive usted?

I am staying at the Hotel España. — Estoy hospedado en el Hotel España. (os-pā-da'-do) (ās-pan'-ya)

I like it. — Me gusta. (goos'-ta)

I don't like it. — No me gusta.

He likes it. — Le gusta.

Give it to me. — Démelo. (dā'-mā-lo)

I think so. — Creo que sí.

I'm in a hurry. — Tengo prisa.

I'm ready. — Estoy listo.

I'm tired. — Estoy cansado.

I'm hungry. (thirsty) (cold) (scared) — Tengo hambre. (sed) (frío) (miedo) (am'-brā) (myā'-do)

Just a moment. — Un momento.

What's that? — ¿Qué es eso?

What do you want? — ¿Qué quiere? (kyā'-rā)

What does that mean? — ¿Qué quiere decir eso?

How do you say that in Spanish? — ¿Cómo se dice eso en español?

Please speak slowly. — Hable despacio, por favor. (dās-pa'-syo)

The masculine form of the adjective generally ends in -o.
The feminine form generally ends in -a.

El está listo. (he is ready.)
Ella está lista. (She is ready.)

Juan está cansado.
Juanita está cansada.

Again. — Otra vez. (bās)

It doesn't matter. — No importa.

Of course. — Claro. Cómo no.

No doubt. — Sin duda.

You're right. — Tiene razón. (tyā'-nä ra-son')

He's wrong. — El no tiene razón.

Wait here. — Espere aquí.

Where are you going? — ¿Adónde va usted?

Where are we going? — ¿Adónde vamos?

Don't bother. — No se moleste. (mo-les'-tä)

It's beautiful. — Está precioso.

Bon voyage! — ¡Buen viaje! (bwän bya'-hä)

Good luck! — ¡Buena suerte! (bwä'-na swär'-tä)

With pleasure. — Con mucho gusto.

Come here. — Venga acá.

Come in. — Entre. or Pase.

Is there...? — ¿Hay...?

Are there...? — ¿Hay...?

Where is...? — ¿Dónde está...?

Where are...? — ¿Dónde están...?

When? — ¿Cuándo?

How much? — ¿Cuánto?

How many? — ¿Cuántos?

Who? — ¿Quién? (kyän)

Which? — ¿Cuál? (kwal)

What? — ¿Qué? (kā)

Why? — ¿Por qué?

Because — Porque

How? — ¿Cómo?

Have you seen...? — ¿Ha visto usted...? (a bees'-to oo-städ')

Although "adiós" means "goodbye," it's often used like "aloha," to greet someone when you're not planning to stop and chat.

GREETINGS & USEFUL EXPRESSIONS
VOCABULARY

according to — según (sā-goon')
after — después de (dās-pwās' dā)
against — contra (kon'-tra)
almost — casi (ka'-see)
also — también (tam-byān')
always — siempre (syām'-prā)
among — entre (ān'-trā)
and — y (ee)
at — a (a)
beautiful — bonito; bello (bo-nèe'-to; bā'-yo)
because — porque (por-kā')
before — antes de (an'-tās dā)
behind — detrás de (dā-tras' dā)
to believe — creer (krā-yār')
below — debajo de (dā-ba'-ho dā)
besides — además (a-dā-mas')
between — entre (ān'-trā)
to bother — molestar (mo-lās-tar')
to come — venir (bā-neer')
day — el día (āl dee'-ya)
during — durante (doo-ran'-tā)
evening — la tarde (la tar'-dā)
far — lejos (lā'-hos)
fear — miedo (myā'-do)
to give — dar (dar)
to go — ir (eer)
goodbye — adiós (a-dyos')
to have — tener (tā-nār')
here — aquí; acá (a-kee'; a-ka')
hunger — hambre (am'-brā)
to know — saber (sa-bār')
to know (to be acquainted with) — conocer (ko-no-sār')
later — luego (lwā'-go)
less — menos (mā-nos)

to live — vivir (bee-beer')

many — muchos (moo'-chos)

more — más (mas)

morning — la mañana (la man-ya'-na)

much — mucho (moo'-cho)

name — el nombre (āl nom'-brā)

near — cerca (sār'-ka)

night — la noche (la no'-chā)

number — el número (āl noo'-mā-ro)

on — en (ān); sobre (so'-brā); encima de (ān-see'-ma dā)

only — sólo (so'-lo)

outside — fuera (fwā'-ra)

please — por favor (por fa-bor')

to please — gustar (goos-tar')

ready — listo (lees'-to)

to room — hospedarse (os-pā-dar'-sā)

to say — decir (dā-seer')

to see — ver (bār)

since — desde (dās'-dā)

slowly — despacio (dās-pa'-syo)

soon — pronto (pron'-to)

Spanish — el español (āl ās-pan-yol')

to speak — hablar (a-blar')

speed — prisa (pree'-sa)

thank you — gracias (gra'-syas)

then — entonces (ān-ton'-sās)

there — allá (a-ya')

thirst — sed (sād)

tired — cansado (kan-sa'-do)

too — demasiado (dā-ma-sya'-do)

trip — el viaje (āl bya'-hā)

to understand — entender (ān-tān-dār')

until — hasta (as'-ta)

very — muy (mooy)

to wait — esperar (ās-pā-rar')

to want — querer (kā-rār')

well — bien (byān)

what — qué (kā)

9

when — cuando (kwan'-do)
where — dónde (don'-dā)
which — cuál (kwal)
who — quién (kyān)
why — por qué (por-kā')
without — sin (seen)
yet — todavía (to-da-bee'-ya)

WEATHER

It's nice weather today. — Hace buen tiempo hoy. (a'-sā
bwān tyām'-po oy)
It's bad weather today. — Hace mal tiempo hoy.
It's cold. — Hace frío.
It's hot. — Hace calor.
It's raining. — Está lloviendo. (ās-ta' yo-byān'-do)
It's windy. — Hace viento.
There's a lot of fog. — Hay mucha niebla. (nyā'-bla)
It's cool there. — Hace tiempo fresco allá.

The definition and pronunciation of **all** words used will be
found in the Glossary.

It's sunny. — Hace sol.
What a beautiful day! — ¿Qué día tan lindo!
It rained yesterday. — Llovió ayer. (yo-byo' a-yār')
The sun is setting. (is rising) — El sol se pone. (se
levanta)
It's beginning to rain. — Empieza a llover. (ām-pyā'-sa a
yo-bār')

WEATHER VOCABULARY

autumn — el otoño (āl o-ton'-yo)
clouds — las nubes (las noo'-bās)
cold — frío (free'-yo)
cool — fresco (frās'-ko)

fog — la niebla (la nyā'-bla)
heat — el calor (āl ka-lor')
lightning — el relámpago (āl rā-lam'-pa-go)
moon — la luna (la loo'-na)
to rain — llover (yo-bār')
rainbow — el arco iris (āl ar'-ko ee'-rees)
sky — el cielo (āl syā'-lo)
snow — la nieve (la nyā'-bā)
spring — la primavera (la pree-ma-bā'-ra)
star — la estrella (la ās-trā'-ya)
storm — la tempestad (la tām-pās-tad')
summer — el verano (āl bā-ra'-no)
sun — el sol (āl sol)
thunder — el trueno (āl trwā'-no)
weather — el tiempo (āl tyām'-po)
wind — el viento (āl byān'-to)
winter — el invierno (āl een-byār'-no)

SIGNS & NOTICES
(for Road Signs, see Driving section)

Abierto — Open
Agua Potable — Drinking Water
Alarma de Incendios — Fire Alarm
Arriba — Up
Ascensor — Elevator
Aviso — Notice; Warning
Baño — Bathroom
Caballeros — Gentlemen
Caja — Cashier's Window
Caliente — Hot
Cerrado — Closed
Correo(s) — Post Office
Cuidado — Caution
Damas — Ladies
Abajo — Down
Empuje — Push

Entrada — Entrance
Escuela — School
Excusado — Toilet
Frío — Cold
Hombres — Men
Iglesia — Church
Información — Information
Jale — Pull
Lavabos — Bathrooms
Libre — Vacant; Free
Mujeres — Women
No Escupir — No Spitting
No Fumar — No Smoking
No Tocar — Don't Touch
Ocupado — Occupied
Oficina — Office
Particular — Private
Peligro — Danger
Precaución — Caution
Privado — Private
Prohibido — Forbidden
Prohibido Entrar — No Entry
Prohibido Fumar — No Smoking
Rebajas — Sale
Reservado — Reserved
Retrete — Toilet
Sala de Espera — Waiting Room
Salida — Exit
Salida de Urgencia — Emergency Exit
Se Alquila — For Rent
Se Vende — For Sale
Señoras — Ladies
Señores — Men
Tire — Pull
Toque el Timbre — Ring the Bell

NUMBERS

one — uno (oo¹-no)
two — dos (dos)
three — tres (träs)
four — cuatro (kwa¹-tro)
five — cinco (seen¹-ko)
six — seis (säs)
seven — siete (syä¹-tä)
eight — ocho (o¹-cho)
nine — nueve (nwä¹-bä)
ten — diez (dyäs)
eleven — once (on¹-sä)
twelve — doce (do¹-sä)
thirteen — trece (trä¹-sä)
fourteen — catorce (ka-tor¹-sä)
fifteen — quince (keen¹-sä)
sixteen — dieciseis (dyäs-ee-säs')
seventeen — diecisiete (dyäs-ee-syä¹-tä)
eighteen — dieciocho (dyäs-ee-o¹-cho)
nineteen — diecinueve (dyäs-ee-nwä¹-bä)

The definition and pronunciation of **all** words used will be found in the Glossary.

twenty — viente (bän¹-tä)
twenty-one — veintiuno (bän-tee-oo¹-no)
twenty-two — veintidós (bän-tee-dos')
thirty — treinta (trän¹-ta)
thirty-one — treinta y uno (trän-ta-ee-oo¹-no)
thirty-five — treinta y cinco (trän-ta-ee-seen¹-ko)
one hundred — cien (syän)
one thousand — mil (meel)
one million — un millón (oon mee-yon)
two hundred — doscientos (do-syän¹-tos)
five hundred — quinientos (keen-yän¹-tos)
first — primero (pree-mä¹-ro)
second — segundo (sä-goon¹-do)

third — tercero (tār-sā'-ro)
fourth — cuarto (kwar'-to)
fifth — quinto (keen'-to)

TIME

What time is it? — ¿Qué hora es? (kā o'-ra ās)
It's one o'clock. — Es la una.
It's two o'clock in the afternoon. — Son las dos de la tarde.
It's a quarter to four. — Son las cuatro menos quince. (keen'-sā) **or** Son quince para las cuatro.
It's six fifteen. — Son las seis y quince. **or** Son las seis y cuarto. (sāees-ee-qwar-to)
It's eleven thirty. — Son las once y media. (on'-sā ee mā'-dya)

The definition and pronunciation of **all** words used will be found in the Glossary.

It's noon. — Es mediodía. (mā-dyo-dee'-ya)
It's midnight. — Es medianoche. (mā-dya-no'-chā)
It's early. — Es temprano.
It's late. — Es tarde.
My watch has stopped. — Se ha parado mi reloj. (rā'-loh)
One minute. Three hours. — Un minuto. Tres horas.
What time does it start? (finish) — ¿A qué hora empieza? (termina) (ām-pyā'-sa)
I will be here four days. — Estaré aquí cuatro días.
When shall we meet? — ¿Cuándo nos reunimos? (rā-oo-nee'-mos)

"Tarde" means both "afternoon" and "evening," as well as "late."

Three days ago. — Hace tres días.

14

TIME VOCABULARY

afternoon — la tarde (la tar'-dā)
day — el día (āl dee'-ya)
evening — la noche (la no'-chā)
hour — la hora (la o'-ra)
midnight — medianoche (ma-dya-no'-chā)
minute — el minuto (āl mee-noo'-to)
month — el mes (āl mās)
morning — la mañana (la ma-nya'-na)
night — la noche (la no'-chā)
noon — mediodía (mā-dyo-dee'-ya)
second — el segundo (āl sā-goon'-do)
time — el tiempo (āl tyām'-po)
tomorrow — mañana (man-ya'-na)
week — la semana (la sā-ma'-na)
year — el año (āl an'-yo)

DAYS & DATES

Monday — el lunes (āl loo'-nās)
Tuesday — el martes (āl mar'-tās)
Wednesday — el miércoles (āl myar-ko-lās)
Thursday — el jueves (āl hwā'-bās)
Friday — el viernes (āl byār'-nās)
Saturday — el sábado (āl s'-ba-do)
Sunday — el domingo (āl do-meen'-go)
January — enero (ā-nā'-ro)
February — febrero (fā-brā'-ro)
March — marzo (mar'-so)
April — abril (a-breel')
May — mayo (ma'-yo)
June — junio (hoo'-nyo)
July — julio (hoo'-lyo)
August — agosto (a-gos'-to)
September — septiembre (sāp-tyām'-brā)
October — octubre (ok-too'-brā)

November — noviembre (no-byām'-brā)

December — diciembre (dee-syām'-brā)

1979 — mil novecientos setenta y nueve (meel no-bā-syān'-tos sā-tān'-tay-nwā'-bā)

the first of June — el primero de junio (āl pree-mār' dā hoo'-nyo)

next spring — la próxima primavera (la prok'-see-ma pree-ma-bā'-ra)

during the winter — durante el invierno (doo-ran'-tā āl een-byār'-no)

last month — el mes pasado (āl mās pa-sa'-do)

next month — el mes próximo (al mas prok'-see-mo)

last year — el año pasado (āl an'-yo pa-sa'-do)

the day after tomorrow — pasado mañana (pa-sa'-do man-ya'-na)

the day before yesterday — anteayer (an-ta-yār)

What's the date? — ¿A como estamos? (a como ās-ta'-mos)

every day — todos los días (to-dòs los dee'-yas)

the day before — el día anterior (āl dee'-ya an-tā-ree-yor')

the day after — el día siguiente (āl dee'-ya see-gyān'-tā)

MONEY

Where's the nearest bank? — ¿Dónde está el banco más cercano?

What time does the bank open? — ¿A qúe hora se abre el banco?

I want to cash a traveler's check. — Quiero cambiar un cheque de viajero. (chā'-kā dā bya-hā'-ro)

What's the exchange rate? — ¿A cómo está el cambio?

Here's my passport. — Aquí tiene mi pasaporte. (a-kee' tyā'-nā)

How would you like it? — ¿Cómo lo quiere? (kyā'-rā)

Please give me some small bills. — Deme algo de billetes pequeños, por favor. (bee-yā'-tās pā-kān'-yos)

Can I change money here at the hotel? — ¿Puedo

cambiar dinero aquí en el hotel?

The definition and pronunciation of **all** words used will be found in the Glossary.

Please count it. — Cuéntelo, por favor. (kwān'-tā-lo)
Sign here. — Firme aquí. (feer'-mā a-kee')
Can I cash a money order here? — ¿Puedo cobrar un giro postal aquí? (hee'-ro po-stal')

MONEY VOCABULARY

bank — el banco (āl ban'-ko)
bill — el billete (āl bee-yā'-tā)
cash — el efectivo (āl ā-fāk-tee'-bo)
to cash — cambiar; cobrar (kam-byar'; ko-brar')
cashier — el cajero (āl ka-hā'-ro)
cashier's window — pagos (pa'-gos)
change (silver) — el cambio; el suelto; el menudo (āl kam'-byo; āl swāl'-to; āl mā-noo'-do)
check — el cheque (āl chā'-kā)
credit card — la tarjeta de crédito (la tar-hā'-ta dā krā'-dee-to)
dollars — los dólares (los do'-lar-ās)
to endorse — endosar (ān-do-sar')
exchange — el cambio (āl kam'-byo)
money — el dinero (āl dee-nā'-ro)
money order — el giro (āl hee'-ro)
pound (currency) — la libra (la lee'-bra)
to sign — firmar (feer-mar')
receipt — el recibo (āl rā-see'-bo)
traveler's check — el cheque de viajero (āl chā'-kā dā bya-hā'-ro)
(bank) window — la ventanilla (la bān-ta-nee'-ya)

The Casa de Cambios (money exchange) and street money changers sometimes offer a better rate of exchange than banks, and often cash traveler's checks free.

17

HOTELS

Where is a good hotel? — ¿Dónde hay un buen hotel?
(don'-dā ay oon bwān o-tāl)

I would like a room for one. (for two) — Quisiera un
cuarto para una persona. (dos personas) (kee-syā'-ra)

How much is a room for two? — ¿Cuánto cuesta un
cuarto para dos?

I would like a single room with bath. — Quisiera un
cuarto con baño para una persona. (kwar'-to kon ban'-yo)

Can I see the room? — ¿Puedo ver el cuarto?

I want a room with a view of the ocean. — Quiero un
cuarto con vista al mar.

The definition and pronunciation of **all** words used will be
found in the Glossary.

Is there hot water? (a shower) — ¿Hay agua caliente?
(una regadera) (ay a'-gwa kal-yān'-tā) (oo'-na
rā-ga-dā'-ra)

How much is this room? — ¿Cuánto es este cuarto?

**Do you have anything less expensive? (larger) (quieter)
(higher up)** — ¿Tiene algo menos caro? (mās grande)
(más tranquilo) (más arriba) (tran-kee'-lo) (a-rre'-ba)

Where is the bathroom? — ¿Dónde está el baño?

What is your rate by the month? (week) (day) —
¿Cuánto cobra por mes? (semana) (día)

Does that include meals? — ¿Están incluídas las comidas?
(éen-klwee'-das)

Fine, I'll take it. — Está bien, lo tomaré.

We will stay one night. — Nos quedamos una noche. (nos
kā-d'-mos oo'-na no'-chā)

I will stay a week. — Me quedo una semana.

I don't know yet. — No sé todavía. (to-da-bee'-ya)

What number is it? — ¿Qué número es?

My key, please. — Mi llave, por favor. **or** La llave, por
favor. (ya'-bā)

I have lost my key. — He perdido mi llave. **or** He perdido la llave. (ā pār-dee⌐-do mee yaᴸ-bā)

Where is the elevator? — ¿Dónde está el ascensor?
(a-sān-sor')

Will you take my baggage to my room? — ¿Me lleva el
equipaje al cuarto? (mā yāᴸ-ba āl ā-kee-paᴸ-hā al kwarᴸ-to)

I need room service. — Necesito servicio de cuarto.

Come in. — Adelante; pase (a-dā-lanᴸ-tā; paᴸ-sā)

Please bring me some ice. — Favor de traerme hielo.
(fa-bor' dā tra-yarᴸ-mā yāᴸ-lo)

If the possessive is understood, it can be omitted.

Please send the maid. — La camarera, por favor.
(ka-ma-rāᴸ-ra)

There are no towels in my room. — No hay toallas en mi
cuarto. (no ay dwayᴸ-yas ān mee kwarᴸ-to)

What's the voltage here? — ¿Cuál es el voltaje aquí?
(kwal ās āl bol-taᴸ-hā a-kee')

I need more soap, please. — Necesito mas jabón, por
favor. (ha-bon')

Do you have laundry service? — ¿Hay servicio de
lavandería? (la-ban-dā-reeᴸ-ya)

Where is the restaurant? — ¿Dónde está el restaurante?

Could you call us a taxi? — ¿Nos puede llamar un taxi?

Do you have a map of the city? — ¿Tiene un mapa de la
ciudad? (syoo-dad')

I'll be back at 3 p.m. — Regreso a las tres de la tarde.

Are there any messages for me? — ¿Hay algún mensaje
para mí? (ay al-goon' mān-sa⌐-hā paᴸ-ra mee)

We are leaving tomorrow. — Salimos mañana.

I'd like my bill, please. — La cuenta, por favor. (la
kwān⌐-ta, por-fa-bor')

Do you accept traveler's checks? — ¿Acceptan cheques
de viajero? (bya-hāᴸ-ro)

Please call me at 6 a.m. — Favor de despertarme a las
seis de la mañana. (dās-pār-tarᴸ-mā a las sāees)

HOTEL VOCABULARY

air conditioned — aire acondicionado (ay⸍-rā
a-kon-dee-syon-a⸍-do)
ashtray — el cenicero (āl sā-nee-sā⸍-ro)
bathroom — el baño (al ban⸍-yo)
bed — la cama (la ka⸍-ma)
bell — el timbre (āl teem⸍-brā)
bill — la cuenta (la kwān⸍-ta)
blanket — la cobija (la ko-bee⸍-ha)
boarding house — la pensión (la pān-syon') la casa de
huéspedes (la ka⸍-sa dā wās⸍-pā-dās)
breakfast — el desayuno (āl dās-ay-oo⸍-no)
chair — la silla (la see⸍-ya)
clean — limpio (leem⸍-pyo)
cold — frío (free⸍-yo)
dining room — el comedor (āl ko-mā-dor')
dinner — la cena (la sā⸍-na)
dirty — sucio (soo⸍-syo)
double bed — la cama matrimonial (la ka⸍-ma
ma-tree-mo-nyal')
elevator — el ascensor (āl a-sān-sor')
glass (drinking) — el vaso (āl ba⸍-so)
ground floor — el primer piso (āl pree-mār pee⸍-so)
heating — la calefacción (la ka-lā-fak-syon')
hot — caliente (kal-yān⸍-tā)
hotel — el hotel (āl o-tāl')
inn — la posada (la po-sa⸍-da)
key — la llave (la ya⸍-bā)
lamp — la lámpara (la lam⸍-pa-ra)
light — la luz (la loos)
manager — el gerente (āl hā-rān⸍-tā)
mattress — el colchón (āl kol-chon')
message — el mensaje; el recado (āl mān-sa⸍-hā; āl
rā-ka⸍-do)
mirror — el espejo (āl ās-pā⸍-ho)
office — la oficina (la o-fee-see⸍-na)

pillow — la almohada (la al-mo-a¹-da)
plug — el enchufe (āl ān-choo¹-fā)
reservation — la reservación (la rā-sār-ba-syon')
sheet — la sábana (la sa¹-ba-na)
shower — la regadera (la rā-ga-dā¹-ra)
soap — el jabón (āl ha-bon)
staircase — la escalera (la ās-ka-lā¹-ra)
table — la mesa (la mā¹-sa)
tap — la llave; el grifo (la ya¹-bā; āl gree¹-fo)
towel — la toalla (la to-ay¹-ya)
washstand — el lavabo (āl la-ba¹-bo)
window — la ventana (la bān-ta¹-na)

Not all lodgings are hotels. Although you can find varia-
tions, here is a list of what the various kinds of lodgings
generally mean:

Hotel — can be found in all price ranges, from "dirt"
cheap to luxury

Pensión — a small family-run hotel that serves meals. You
can have a room **con comida** (with meals) or **sin
comida** (without meals)

Hospedaje — like a pensión, but generally doesn't serve
meals

Casa de huéspedes — like a rooming house
Alojamiento — also like a rooming house

Casa familiar ⎫
Hostería ⎬ — generally like a rooming house, but
Residenciá ⎭   sometimes serves meals

TELEPHONE

Where's a telephone? — ¿Dónde hay un teléfono?
(tā-lā¹-fo-no)
Do I need to use tokens? — ¿Necesito usar fichas?
(fee¹-chas)
I want to make a telephone call. — Quiero telefonear.
(tā-lā-fo-nā-yar')

21

Do you speak English? — ¿Habla usted inglés?

Operator, I want to make a long distance call. — Señorita, quiero hacer una llamada de larga distancia. (ya-ma'-da) (dees-tan'-sya)

I want to call Los Angeles. — Quiero telefonear a Los Angeles. (an'-hā-lās)

How much does it cost? — ¿Cuánto cuesta?

The definition and pronunciation of **all** words used will be found in the Glossary.

Can I dial the number? — ¿Puedo marcar el número? (pwā'-do mar-kar' āl noo'-mā-ro)

May I speak to...? — ¿Puedo hablar con...?

He (She) is not in. — El (Ella) no está.

When will he be back? — ¿Cuándo volverá? (kwan'-do bol-bā-ra')

They don't answer. — No contestan.

Deposit your coins. — Deposite sus monedas. (da-po'-see-tā soos mo-nā'-das)

Hello? — ¿Diga?; ¿Bueno?

Who's speaking? — ¿Quién habla?

Please speak more slowly. — Hable más despacio, por favor. (dās-pa'-syo)

When using the telephone directory, remember that in the Spanish alphabet the "CH" listings come after the "C" listings, the "LL" after the "L", and the "Ñ" after the "N."

The line is busy. — La línea está ocupada. (o-koo-pa'-da)

I need a telephone book. — Necesito una guía telefónica. (gee'-ya tā-lā-fo'-nee-ka)

TELEPHONE VOCABULARY

call — la llamada (la ya-ma'-da)

to call — llamar (ya-mar')

to dial — marcar (mar-kar')

22

directory — la guía telefónica (la gee'-ya tä-lä-fo'-nee-ka)
long distance — larga distancia (lar'-ga dees-tan'-sya)
number — el número (äl noo'-mä-ro)
operator — la telefonista; la señorita (la tä-lä-fo-nees'-ta; la sän-yo-ree'-ta)
receiver — el auricular (äl aoo-ree-koo-lar')
token — la ficha (la fee'-cha)
wrong number — el número equivocado (äl noo'-mä-ro ä-kee-bo-ka'-do)

TAXI & BUS

Call me a taxi, please. — Llame un taxi, por favor. (ya'-mä oon tak'-see)

Where can I get a taxi? — ¿Dónde puedo coger un taxi? (ko-här')

Are you free, driver? — ¿Está usted libre, chofer?

I want to go to the Hotel Colonial. — Quiero ir al Hotel Colonial. (o-täl' ko-lo-nyal')

How much is it to the ruins? — ¿Cuánto es a las ruinas? (rwee'-nas)

Take me to the airport, please. — Lléveme al aeropuerto, por favor. (yä'-bä-mä al a-ä-ro-pwär'-to)

The definition and pronunciation of **all** words used will be found in the Glossary.

For taxis, establish the price in advance.

Go straight ahead. — Siga derecho. (see'-ga dä-rä'-cho)
I want to get out here. — Quiero bajar aquí. (ba-har')
Wait for me here. — Espéreme aquí. (äs-pär'-ä-mä)
I'm in a hurry. — Tengo prisa. (pree'-sa)
A little further on. — Un poco más adelante. (a-dä-lan'-tä)
Here are my bags. — Aquí tiene mi equipaje. (ä-kee-pa'-hä)

More slowly, please. — Más despacio, por favor. (däs-pa'-syo)

How much do I owe you? — ¿Cuánto le debo?

Does the bus stop here? — ¿Para el autobús aquí? (aoo-to-boos')

Which bus goes to the market? — ¿Cuál autobús va al mercado? (kwal)

Does this bus go downtown? — ¿Va este autobús al centro?

I want the bus to Taxco. — Quiero el autobús a Taxco. (tas'-ko)

Get on the bus here. — Suba el autobús aquí. (soo'-ba)

Get off the bus here. — Baje aquí. (ba'-hä)

Where's the bus station? — ¿Dónde está la estación de autobuses? (äs-ta-syon')

The bus to Acapulco leaves from Gate 7. — El autobús a Acapulco sale del Andén Siete. (a-ka-pool'-ko) (an-dän' syä'-tä)

When is the next bus? — ¿Cuándo sale el siguiente autobús? (see-gyän'-tä)

When is the last bus? — ¿Cuándo sale el último autobús? (ool'-tee-mo)

How long does it take? — ¿Cuánto tarda?

The buses run every hour. — Hay autobuses cada hora.

What city is this? — ¿Cuál ciudad es ésta? (syoo-dad')

The window doesn't open. (close) — No abre (cierra) la ventana. (a'-brä) (syä'-rra)

Latin countries often have two classes of bus service, the second class being cheaper and less comfortable.

TAXI & BUS VOCABULARY

to arrive — llegar (yä-gar')
bus — el autobús; el camión (äl aoo-to-boos'
bus stop — la parada de autobuses (la pa-ra'-da dä aoo-to-boo'-säs)

cathedral — la catedral (la ka-tā-dral')
to change — cambiar (kam-byar')
conductor — el cobrador (āl ko-bra-dor')
downtown — el centro (āl sān'-tro)
driver — el chofer (āl cho'-fār)
fare — la tarifa (la ta-ree'-fa)
first class — primera clase (pree-mā'-ra kla'-sā)
to leave — salir (sa-leer')
market — el mercado (āl mār-ka'-do)
museum — el museo (āl moo-sā'-yo)
one-way ticket — el boleto de ida (āl bo-lā'-to dā ee'-da)
railway station — la estación de ferrocarriles (la ās-ta-syon' dā fā-rro-ka-rree'-lās)
round-trip ticket — el boleto de ida y vuelta (āl bo-lā'-to dā ee'-da ee bwāl'-ta)
ruins — las ruinas (las rwee'-nas)
second class — segunda clase (sā-goon'-da kla'-sā)
station — la estación (la ās-ta-syon')
taxi — el taxi (āl tak'-see)
ticket — el boleto (āl bo-lā'-to)
ticket window — la taquilla (la ta-kee'-ya)
tip — la propina (la pro-pee'-na)
toilet — el servicio; el baño (āl sār-bee'-syo; āl ba'-nyo)
to turn — doblar (do-blar')
university — la universidad (la oo-nee-bar-see-dad')
waiting room — la sala de espera (la sa'-la dā ās-pa'-ra)

EATING OUT

I'm hungry. — Tengo hambre. (am'-brā)
I'm thirsty. — Tengo sed. (sād)
Where's a good restaurant? — ¿Dónde hay un buen restaurante? (rās-taoo-ran'-tā)
Let's eat now. — Comamos ahora. (ko-ma'-mos a-o'-ra)
Do you want to eat now? — ¿Quiere usted comer ahora? (ko-mār')

I'd like a table for 4. — Quisiera una mesa para cuatro. (kee-syā'-ra) (kwa'-tro)

The definition and pronunciation of **all** words used will be found in the Glossary.

Is there a menu? — ¿Hay un menú? (mā-noo')

I want a table on the patio. — Quiero una mesa en el patio. (kyā'-ro) (pa'-tyo)

Near the window, please. — Cerca de la ventana, por favor. (sār'-ka) (bān-ta'-na)

Where is the waiter? (waitress) — ¿Dónde está el camarero? (la camarera) (ka-ma-rā'-ro) (la ka-ma-rā'-ra)

Is there a wine list? — ¿Hay una lista de vinos?

At what time is breakfast? (lunch) (dinner) — ¿A qué hora es el desayuno? (el almuerzo) (la comida) (dās-ay-yoo'-no) (āl al-mwār'-so) (la ko-mee'-da)

I want to wash my hands. — Quiero lavarme las manos.

Over there. (Downstairs) — Por allá. (Abajo) (a-ya') (a-ba'-ho)

Dinner is served. — La comida está servida. (sār-bee'-da)

A glass of plain water, please. — Un vaso de agua natural, por favor. (a'-gwa na-too-ral')

I'll have the set meal. — Quiero la comida corrida.

We'll order a la carte. — Pediremos a la carta. (pā-deer-ā'-mos)

What do you recommend? — ¿Qué recomienda usted? (rā-ko-myān'-da)

What would you like? — ¿Qué desea? (kā dā-sā'-yā)

Please bring an ashtray. — Traiga un cenicero, por favor. (tray'-ga oon sā-nee-sā'-ro)

We have no napkins. — No tenemos servilletas. (sār-bee-yā'-tas)

What's the specialty of the house? — ¿Cuál es la especialidad de la casa? (kwal) (ā-spā-see-ya-lee-dad')

What is this? — ¿Qué es ésto?

I'd like to try that. — Quisiera probar eso. (kee-syā'-ra)

No salt, please. — Sin sal, por favor.

No hot sauce. —Sin picante. (seen pee-can'-tā)

I want my coffee now. —Quiero mi café ahora. (a-o'-ra)

I take milk and sugar. —Tomo leche y azucar. (lā'-chā ee a-soo'-kar)

The coffee is cold. —El café está frío.

This isn't clean. —Esto no está limpio. (ās'-tā no ās-ta' leem'-pyo)

May I have another fork? —¿Me da otro tenedor? (tā-nā-dor')

The milk is sour. —La leche está agria. (a-gree-ya)

Do you want more coffee? —¿Quiere más café?

I didn't order this. —No pedí ésto.

I'd like a cocktail, please. —Quisiera un cóctel, por favor. (kee-syā'-ra oon kok'-tāl)

Do you serve wine by the glass? —¿Sirven vino por vaso?

The wine is too warm. —El vino está demasiado caliente. (dā-ma-syā'-do kal-yān'-tā)

A half bottle of white wine, please. (red wine) —Media botella de vino blanco, por favor. (vino tinto) (mā'-dya bo-tā'-ya)

Bring me some ice. —Traígame un poco de hielo. (tray'-ga-mā) (yā'-lo)

Do you like fish? (meat) (desserts) —¿Le gusta el pescado? (la carne) (los postres) (lā goos'-ta āl pās-ka'-do) (la kar'-nā) (los pos'-trās)

I would like some fruit. —Me gustaría alguna fruta. (goos-ta-ree'-ya)

He doesn't eat desserts. —El no come postres.

The check, please. —La cuenta, por favor.

Where do I pay? —¿Dónde pago?

At the cashier's window. —En la caja. (ka'-ha)

Is service included? —¿Está incluído el servicio? (een-klwee'-do)

I've already paid. —Ya he pagado.; Ya pagué. (ya ā pa-ga'-do; ya pa-gā')

I left a tip on the table. —Dejé la propina en la mesa. (dā'-hā)

There's an error in my bill. — Hay un error en mi cuenta.

It's alright now. — Ahora está bien.

We enjoyed the meal, thank you. — Nos gustó la comida, gracias. (nos goos-to')

MENU TRANSLATOR

APERITIVOS; ENTREMESES — Appetizers
(a-pä-ree-tee'-bos); (än-trä-mä'-säs)

aceitunas — olives (a-sa-too'-nas)

alcachofas — artichokes (al-ka-cho'-fas)

anchoas — anchovies (an-cho'-as)

arenque — herring (a-rän'-kä)

camarones — shrimp (ka-ma-ro'-näs)

ceviche — marinated fish (sä-bee'-chä)

encurtidos — pickles (än-koor-tee'-dos)

entremeses — hors d'oeuvres; appetizers (än-trä-mä'-säs)

_____

The definition and pronunciation of **all** words used will be found in the Glossary.

fiambres — cold cuts (fyam'-bräs)

hígado — liver (ee'-ga-do)

ostras — oysters (os'-tras)

SOPAS — Soups (so'-pas)

caldo — chicken broth (kal'-do)

gazpacho — a chilled vegetable soup (gas-pa'-cho)

sopa — soup (so'-pa)

sopa clara — consomme (so'-pa kla'-ra)

sopa de ajo — garlic soup (so'-pa dä a'-ho)

sopa de albóndigas — meatball soup (so'-pa dä al-bon-dee'-gas)

sopa de legumbres — vegetable soup (so'-pa dä lä-goom'-bräs)

PESCADO — Fish (päs-ka'-do)

abulón — abalone (a-boo-lon')

almejas — clams (al-mā^L-has)

anguilas — eel (an-gee^L-las)

atún — tuna (a-toon')

calamares — squid (ka-la-ma^L-räs)

camarones — shrimp (ka-ma-ro^L-näs)

cangrejo — crab (kan-grä^L-ho)

caracoles — snails (ka-ra-ko^L-läs)

gambas — large shrimp (gam^L-bas)

huachinango — red snapper (wa-chee-nang^L-go)

langosta — lobster (lan-gos^L-ta)

lenguado — sole (län-gwa^L-do)

mariscos — shellfish (ma-rees^L-kos)

mero — sea bass (mā^L-ro)

ostras — oysters (os^L-tras)

paella — a rice dish with assorted meats and seafood (pa-ä^L-ya)

pescado — fish (päs-ka^L-do)

pulpo — octopus (pool^L-po)

CARNES Y AVES — Meats and Poultry (kar^L-näs ee a^L-bäs)

barbacoa — barbecue (bar-ba-ko^L-a)

bistec — beef steak (bees^L-täk)

cabrito — kid (ka-bree^L-to)

carne — meat (kar^L-nä)

carnero — mutton (kar-nä^L-ro)

cerdo — pork (sär^L-do)

chuletas — cutlets or chops (choo-lä^L-tas)

conejo — rabbit (ko-nä^L-ho)

corazón — heart (ko-ra-son')

costillas — ribs (kos-tee^L-yas)

filete — fillet (fee-lä^L-tä)

guajalote — turkey (in Mexico); pavo in other countries (gwa-ho-lo^L-tä)

guisado — stew (gee-sa^L-do)

hígado — liver (ee^L-ga-do)

jamón — ham (ha-mon')

lechón — suckling pig (lā-chon')
milanesa — breaded steak (mee-la-nā'-sa)
pato — duck (pa'-to)
pavo — turkey (pa'-bo)
pechuga — breast (pā-choo'-ga)
pollo — chicken (po'-yo)
pollo asado — roast chicken (po'-yo a-sa'-do)
res — beef (rās)
salchicha — sausage (sal-chee'-cha)
ternera — veal (tār-nā'-ra)
tocino — bacon (to-see'-no)

VEGETABLES; LEGUMBRES — Vegetables
   (bā-hā-ta'-lās; lā-goom'-brās)
apio — celery (a'-pyo)
arroz — rice (a-ros')
betabel (remolacha) — beet (bā-ta-bāl')
calabaza — squash; zucchini (ka-la-ba'-sa)
cebolla — onion (sā-boy'-a)
champiñones — mushrooms (cyham-peen-yo'-nās)
col — cabbage (kol)
coliflor — cauliflower (ko-lee-flor')
elotes — corn on the cob (ā-lo'-tās)
ensalada — salad (ān-sa-la'-da)
favas — lima beans (fa'-bas)
frijoles — beans (free-ho'-lās)
hongos — mushrooms (on'-gos)
lechuga — lettuce (lā-choo'-ga)
lentejas — lentils (lān-tā'-has)
maíz — corn
papa — potato (pa'-pa)
pepino (cohombro) — cucumber (pā-pee'-no)
perejil — parsley (pā-rā-heel')
rábano — radish (ra'-ba-no)
repollo — cabbage (rā-po'-yo)
tomate — tomato (to-ma'-tā)
zanahoria — carrot (sa-na-o'-ree-a)

FRUTAS — Fruits (froo'-tas)
albaricoque — apricot (al-ba-ree-ko'-kā)
almendra — almond (al-mān'-dra)
castaña — chestnut (kas-tan'-ya)
cereza — cherry (sā-rā'-sa)
chabacano — apricot (chya-ba-ka'-no)
ciruela — plum (seer-wā'-la)
coco — coconut (ko'-ko)
dátiles — dates (da'-tee-lās)
durazno — peach (doo-ras'-no)
frambuesa — raspberry (fram-bwā'-sa)
fresa — strawberry (frā'-sa)
frutas — fruit (froo'-tas)
higo — fig (ee'-go)
lima — lime (lee'-ma)
limón — lemon (lee-mon')
manzana — apple (man-sa'-na)
melón — melon (mā-lon')
membrillo — quince (mām-bree'-yo)
naranja — orange (na-ran'-ha)
nueces — nuts (nwā'-sās)
pasa — raisin (pa'-sa)
pera — pear (pā'-ra)
piña — pineapple (peen'-ya)
plátano — banana (pla'-ta-no)
sandía — watermelon (san-dee'-ya)
toronja (pomelo) — grapefruit (to-ron'-ha)
uva — grape (oo'-ba)

POSTRES — Desserts (pos'-trās)
almíbar — syrup (al-mee'-bar)
chocolate — chocolate (cho-ko-la'-tā)
crema — cream (krā'-ma)
dulces — sweets (dool'-sās)
flan — a kind of custard (flan)
fresa — strawberry (frā'-sa)
galletas — cookies (ga-yā'-tas)

helado — ice cream (ā-la^L-do)
nata — cream (na^L-ta)
pastel — cake (pas-tāl')
postre — dessert (pos^L-trā)
turrón — nougat (too-rron')
vainilla — vanilla (bay-nee^L-ya)

BEBIDAS — Beverages (bā-bee^L-das)
agua mineral — mineral water (a^L-gwa mee-nā-ral')
bebida — beverage; drink (bā-bee^L-da)
café — coffee (ka-fā')
café con leche — coffee with milk (ka-fā' kon lā^L-chā)
café negro — black coffee (ka-fā' nā^L-gro)
cerveza — beer (sār-bā^L-sa)
coñac — brandy (kon^L-yak)
ginebra — gin (hee-nā^L-bra)
horchata — "almond milk" (or-cha^L-ta)
jerez — sherry (hā-rās')
jugo — juice (hoo^L-go)
jugo de naranja — orange juice (hoo^L-go dā na-ran^L-ha)
leche — milk (lā^L-chā)
limonada — lemonade (lee-mo-na^L-da)
oporto — port (o-por^L-to)
ron — rum (ron)
sangría — mildly alcoholic fruit punch (san-gree^L-ya)
té — tea (tā)
vino — wine (bee^L-no)

Varios — Miscellaneous

aceite — oil (a-sā^L-tā)
ajo — garlic (a^L-ho)
azúcar — sugar (a-soo^L-kar)
bocadillo — sandwich (bo-ka-dee^L-yo)
bolillo — a kind of roll (bo-lee^L-yo)
enchilada — meat or cheese rolled in a soft tortilla &
  baked in sauce (ān-chee-la^L-da)

huevo — egg (wā-bo)
mantequilla — butter (man-tā-kee-ya)
margarina — margarine (mar-ga-ree-na)
mayonesa — mayonnaise (ma-yo-nā-sa)
mermelada — jelly (mār-mā-la-da)
miel — honey (myāl)
mostaza — mustard (mos-sta-sa)
pan — bread (pan)
pimienta — pepper (pee-myān-ta)
queso — cheese (kā-so)
sal — salt (sal)
salsa — sauce (sal-sa)
salsa de tomate — catsup (sal-sa dā to-ma-tā)
taco — meat & vegetables on a crisp, rolled tortilla (ta-ko)
tamale — seasoned ground meat wrapped in cornmeal
    dough & steamed (ta-ma-lā)
torta — sandwich made on a bolillo (tor-ta)
tortilla — an unleavened, unsweetened corn pancake, used
    in many dishes (tor-tee-ya)
tortilla a la española — omelet (tor tee' ya a la
    ās-pan-yo-la)

OTHER RESTAURANT VOCABULARY

ashtray — el cenicero (āl sā-nee-sa-ro)
baked — al horno (al or-no)
baked — al horno (al or-no)
bar — el bar (al bar)
bathroom — el baño; el servicio (āl ban-yo; āl
    sār-bee-syo)
bill — la cuenta (la kwān-ta)
bottle — la botella (la botā-ya)
cashier — el cajero (āl ka-hā-ro)
cigarettes — los cigarrillos (los see-ga-rree-yos)
cold — frío (free-yo)
cork — el corcho (āl kor-cho)
cup — la taza (la ta-sa)

33

fork — el tenedor (āl tā-nā-dor')

fried — frito (free^L-to)

glass — el vaso (āl ba^L-so)

grilled — a la plancha; a la parrilla (a la plan^L-cha; a la pa-rree^L-ya)

hot — caliente (kal-yān^L-tā)

knife — el cuchillo (āl koo-chee^L-yo)

marinated — en escabeche (ān ās-ka-bā^L-chā)

matches — los cerillos (los sā-ree^L-yos)

meal — la comida (la ko-mee^L-da)

medium (cooked) — medio cocido (mā^L-dyo ko-see^L-do)

menu — el menú (āl mā-noo')

napkin — la servilleta (la sār-bee-yā^L-ta)

plate — el plato (āl pla^L-to)

rare — poco hecho (po^L-ko ā^L-cho)

raw — crudo (kroo^L-do)

restaurant — el restaurante (āl rās-taoo-ran^L-tā)

roasted — asado (a-sa^L-do)

service — el servicio (āl sār-bee^L-syo)

shoeshine man — el limpiabotas (āl leem-pya-bo^L-tās)

smoked — ahumado (a-oo-ma^L-do)

spoon — la cuchara (la koo-cha^L-ra)

stuffed — relleno (rā-yā^L-no)

table — la mesa (la mā^L-sa)

tablecloth — el mantel (āl man-tāl')

tip — la propina (la pro-pee^L-na)

toasted — tostado (tos-ta^L-do)

toothpick — el palillo (āl pa-lee^L-yo)

vegetarian — vegetariano (bā-hā-ta-ree-ya^L-no)

waiter — el camarero (al ka-ma-ra-ro)

waitress — la camarera; la mesera (la ka-ma-rā-ra; la ma-sā-ra)

water jug — la garrafa (la ga-rra^L-fa)

well done — bien cocido (byān ko-see^L-do)

SHOPPING

I want to go shopping. — Quiero ir de compras.
Where are the best shops? — ¿Dónde están las mejores
tiendas? (mā-ho'-rās)
Where can I buy...? — ¿Dónde puedo comprar...?
What time do the stores open? — ¿A qué hora se abren
las tiendas? (a kā o'-ra sā a'-brān las tyān'-das)
**Where is there a department store? (a drug store) (a
shoe repair shop)** — ¿Dónde hay un almacén? (una
farmacia) (una zapatería) (al-ma-sān') (far-ma'-sya)
(sa-pa-tā-ree'-ya)
A stationery store. — Una papelería. (pa-pā-lā-ree'-ya)
A dressmaker. — Una modista. (mo-dees'-ta)

The definition and pronunciation of **all** words used will be
found in the Glossary.

A tailor shop. — Una sastrería. (sas-trā-ree'-ya)
A jewelry store. — Una joyería. (hoy-ā-ree'-ya)
May I help you? — ¿En qué puedo servirle? (sār-beer'-lā)
What do you wish? — ¿Qué desea?
Where is the market? — ¿Dónde está el mercado?
I'd like to see a shirt. (dress) (skirt) (blouse) — Quisiera
ver una camisa. (un vestido) (una falda) (una blusa)
What size? — ¿Qué talla? (tay'-ya)
Do you have a larger (smaller) size? — ¿Tiene una talla
más grande (pequeño)? (pā-kān'-yo)
Do you have it in white? (black) (blue) (red) — ¿Lo tiene
en blanco? (negro) (azul) (rojo) (a-sool') (ro'-ho)
Do you have any others? — ¿Hay otros?
I want to try this on. — Quiero probármelo.
(pro-bar'-mā-lo)
It doesn't look good on me. — No me queda bien.
I'll take this one. — Me quedo con éste.
How much is it? — ¿Cuánto es?
Will you write the price? — ¿Podría escribir el precio?
(po-dree'-ya ās-kree-beer' āl prā'-syo)

I need a pair of sandals. — Necesito un par de hauraches (sandalias). (wa-ra'-chãs)

These are too tight. (loose) (big) — Estos son demasiado apretados. (flojos) (grandes) (dã-ma-sya'-do a-prã-ta'-dos) (flo-hos)

Try this pair. — Pruebe este par. (prwã'-bã)

I'd like to see some necklaces. (bracelets) (rings) — Quisiera ver unos collares. (unas pulseras) (unos anillos) (ko-ya'-rãs)

Do you have some in gold? (silver) — ¿Tiene algunos de oro? (plata)

I'm just looking. — Sólo estoy mirando.

How many carats is this? — ¿De cuántos quilates es ésto? (kee-la'-tãs)

Can you send it to . . . ? — ¿Puede mandarlo a . . . ?

Will you wrap it please? — ¿Lo envuelve por favor? (ãn-bwãl'-bã)

I need some toothpaste. — Necesito pasta dentífrica. (dãn-tee'-free-ka)

A toothbrush. — Un cepillo de dientes. (sã-pee'-yo) (dyãn'-tãs)

Razor blades. — Hojas de afeitar. (o'-has dã a-fã-tar')

Toilet paper. — Papel higiénico. (pa-pãl' ee-hyãn'-ee-ko)

Shampoo. — Champú.

Shoe laces. — Cordones de zapato.

Band-aids. — Venditas.

Contraceptives. — Contraceptivos. (kon-tra-sãp-tee'-bos)

Where's a bookstore? — ¿Dónde está una librería? (lee-brã-ree'-ya)

Do you have books (magazines) newspapers) in English? — ¿Tiene libros (revistas) (períodicos) en inglés?

I want to buy souvenirs. — Quiero comprar recuerdos. (rã-kwãr'-dos)

I want a hat. (bathing suit) (shawl) — Quiero un sombrero. (traje de baño) (chal)

May I have a receipt? — ¿Me puede dar un recibo? (rã-see'-bo)

I don't have change. — No tengo cambio. (kam'-byo)

It's too expensive. — Es demasiado caro. (dā-mā-sya'-do ka'-ro)

Do you have anything cheaper? — ¿Tiene algo más barato?

Where do they sell leather goods? — ¿Dónde venden artículos de piel? (ar-tee'-koo-los dā pyāl)

I want a leather jacket, large size. — Quiero una chaqueta de piel, de tamaño grande. (cha-kā'-ta) (ta-man'-yo)

I (don't) like it. — (No) me gusta. (goos'-ta)

Do you accept traveler's checks? — ¿Acepta cheques de viajero? (chā'-kās dā bya-ha'-ro)

I'll pay cash. — Pagaré al contado. (pa-ga-rā')

SHOPPING VOCABULARY

bakery — la panadería (la pa-na-dā-ree'-ya)

barber shop — la pcluquería (la pā-loo-kā-ree'-ya)

battery — la batería (la ba-tā-ree'-ya)

belt — el cinto (āl seen'-to)

blouse — la blusa (la bloo'-sa)

book — el libro (āl lee'-bro)

book store — la librería (la lee-brā-ree'-ya)

bracelet — la pulsera (la pool-sā'-ra)

candy — los dulces (los dool'-sās)

candy store — la dulcería (la dool-sā-ree'-ya)

cap — la gorra (la go'-rra)

cigar — el puro (āl poo'-ro)

counter — el mostrador (āl mos-tra-dor')

department store — el almacén (āl al-ma-sān')

discount — la rebaja (la ra-ba'-ha); el descuento (āl dās-kwān'-to)

doll — la muñeca (la moon-yā'-ka)

dress — el vestido (āl bās-tee'-do)

dressmaker — la modista (la mo-dees'-ta)

drugstore — la farmacia (la far-ma'-sya)

dry cleaner — la tintorería (la teen-tor-rār-ree'-ya)

earrings — los aretes (los a-rā'-tās)

envelope — el sobre (āl so'-brā)

florist — el florero (āl flo-rā'-ro)

gift — el regalo (āl rā-ga'-lo)

gold — el oro (āl o'-ro)

guide book — la guía (la gee'-ya)

hat — el sombrero (āl som-brā'-ro)

hat store — la sombrerería (la som-brā-rā-ree'-ya)

heel — el tacón (āl ta-kon')

ink — la tinta (la teen'-ta)

jacket — la chaqueta (la cha-kā'-ta)

jade — el jade (āl ha'-dā) .

jewelry store — la joyería (la hoy-ā-ree'-ya)

laundry — la lavandería (la la-ban-dā-ree'-ya)

liquor store — la tienda de licores (la tyān'-da dā lee-ko'-rās)

lotion — la loción (la lo-syon')

magazine — la revista (la rā-bees'-ta)

map — el mapa (āl ma'-pa)

market — el mercado (āl mār-ka'-do)

matches — los fósforos (los fos'-fo-ros)

nail file — la lima de uñas (la lee'-ma dā oon'-yas)

necklace — el collar (āl ko-yar')

needle — la aguja (la a-goo'-ha)

newspaper — el periódico (āl pā-ree-o'-dee-ko)

pants — los pantalones (los pan-ta-lo'-nās)

pen — la pluma (la ploo'-ma)

pencil — el lápiz (āl la'-pees)

photo store — la tienda de fotografía (la tyān'-da dā fo-to-gra-fee'-ya)

pin — el alfiler (āl al-fee-lār')

pipe — la pipa (la pee'-pa)

pipe cleaners — las escobillas (las ās-ko-bee'-yas)

pottery — la loza (la lo'-sa)

razor blades — las hojas de afeitar (las o'-has dā a-fa-tar')

ring — el anillo (āl a-nee'-yo)

sale — la venta (la bān'-ta)

scissors — las tijeras (las tee-hā'-ras)
shampoo — el champú (āl cham-poo')
shawl — el chal (āl chal)
shirt — la camisa (la ka-mee'-sa)
shoe store — la zapatería (la sa-pa-tā-ree'-ya)
shoes — los zapatos (los sa-pa'-tos)
silver — la plata (la pla'-ta)
skirt — la falda (la fal'-da)
soap — el jabón (āl ha-bon')
sole — la suela (la swā'-la)
stationery store — la papelería (la pa-pā-lā-ree'-ya)
straw — la paja (la pa'-ha)
suit — el traje (āl tra'-hā)
tailor shop — la sastrería (la sas-trā-ree'-ya)
thread — el hilo (āl ee'-lo)
tobacco — el tabaco (āl ta-ba'-ko)
tobacconist — el tabaquería (la ta-ba-kā-ree'-ya)
tooth brush — el cepillo de dientes (āl sa-pee'-yo dā dyān'-tās)
tooth paste — la pasta dentífrica (la pas'-ta dān-tee'-free-ka)
toy — el juguete (āl hoo-gā'-tā)
umbrella — el paraguas (āl pa-ra'-gwas)
wallet — la cartera (la kar-tā'-ra)
watch — el reloj (āl rā'-lo)
watchmaker — el relojero (āl rā-lo-hā'-ro)
writing paper — el papel de escribir (āl pa-pāl' dā ās kree-beer')

DRIVING

I would like to rent a car. — Quisiera alquilar un coche. (kee-syā'-ra al-kee-lar' oon ko'-chā)
How much is it per day? — ¿Cuánto cuesta por día?
How much is the insurance per day? — ¿Cuánto es el seguro al día? (sā-goo'-ro)
Where's a gas station? — ¿Dónde está una estación de gasolina? (es-tā-cion')

Fill it up, please. — Llénelo, por favor. (yā'-nā-lo)

I'd like premium. (regular) — Quisiera superior. (ordinario) (soo-pā-ryor') (or-dee-na'-ree-o)

The definition and pronunciation of **all** words used will be found in the Glossary.

I want 30 liters. — Quiero treinta litros. (trān'-ta)

Check the oil. (the water) (the tires) — Revise el aceite. (el agua) (las llantas) (a-sā'-tā) (yan'-tas)

I need some air too. — Necesito aire también (ay'-rā tam-byān')

Please wash the car. (the windshield) — Lave el coche, por favor. (el parabrisas) (pa-ra-bree'-sas)

I need a mechanic. — Necesito un mecánico. (mā-ka'-nee-ko)

My car has broken down. — Mi coche se ha estropeado. (ās-tro-pā-ya'-do)

The car won't start. — El coche no arranca.

Can you fix . . . ? — ¿Puede reparar . . . ?

How long will it take? — ¿Cuánto tardará?

How much will it cost? — ¿Cuánto costará?

I don't know what the matter is. — No sé lo que tiene.

I think it's . . . — Creo que es . . .

There's a rattle. — Hay un tra-kā-tā'-o)

I have a flat tire. — Tengo una llanta desinflada. (yan'-ta dās-een-fla'-da)

The radiator is leaking. — Gotea el radiador. (go-tā'-a)

I need a road map. — Necesito un mapa de carreteras. (ka-rrā-tā'-ras)

Is this the road to Monterey? — ¿Es éste el camino a Monterey?

It's that way. — Está por allá.

Is there an expressway? — ¿Hay autopista? (aoo-to-pees'-ta)

Is the road good? — ¿Es bueno el camino?

It isn't far. — No está lejos. (lā'-hos)

Can I park here? — ¿Puedo estacionar aquí? (ās-ta-syo-nar')

I want to leave the car overnight. — Quiero dejar el coche durante la noche. (dā-har')

How do I get to Guadalajara? — ¿Cómo llego a Guadalajara? (yā'-go a wa-da-la-ha'-ra)

Straight ahead. Turn right. Turn left. — Todo derecho. Doble a la derecha. Doble a la izquierda. (dā-rā'-cho) (ees-kyār'-da)

There's been an accident. — Ha habido un accidente. (a a-bee'-do oon ak-see-dān'-tā)

Here is my driver's license. — Aquí tiene mi licencia de manejar. (lee-sān'-sya dā ma-nā-har')

I'd like an interpreter. — Quisiera un intérprete.

ROAD SIGNS

Aduana — Customs
Alto — Stop
Aparcamiento — Parking
Autopista — Expressway
Camino Cerrado — Road Closed
Camino Sinuoso — Winding Road
Ceda el Paso — Yield Right of Way
Conserve su Derecha — Keep Right
Cuidado — Caution
Curva — Curve
Despacio — Slow
Desviación — Detour
Direccion Unica — One Way
Escuela — School
Estacionamiento — Parking
Estacionamiento Prohibido — No Parking
Ferrocarril — Railroad
Glorieta — Traffic Circle
Obras — Men Working
Pare — Stop
Paso de Ganado — Cattle Crossing
No Hay Paso — No Thoroughfare

Peatones — Pedestrians
Peligro — Danger
Pendiente — Steep Hill
Prohibido el Paso — No Entry
Puente Angosto — Narrow Bridge
Velocidad Máxima — Speed Limit
Virajes — Winding Road

DRIVING VOCABULARY

accelerator — el acelerador (āl a-sāl-ā-ra-dor')
back (direction) — detrós (dā-tras')
battery — la batería (la ba-tā-ree'-ya)
border — la frontera (la fron-tā'-ra)
brakes — los frenos (los frā'-nos)
bridge — el puente (āl pwăn'-tā)
car — el coche (āl ko'-chā)
carburetor — el carburador (āl kar-boo-ra-dor')
clutch — el embrague (āl ăm-bra'-gā)
curve — la curva (la koor'-ba)
cylinder — el cilindro (āl see-leen'-dro)
dangerous — peligroso (pā-lee-gro'-so)
distributor — el distribuidor (āl dees-tree-bwee-dor')
to drive — manejar (ma-nā-har')
driver — el conductor; el chófer (āl kon-dook-tor' cho'-fār)
driver's licence — la licencia de manejar (la lee-sān'-sya dā ma-nā-har')
engine — el motor (āl mo-tor')
exhaust — el tubo de escape (āl tubo de escape (āl too'-bo dā ās-ka'-pā)
fanbelt — la correa del ventilador (la ko-rrā'-ya dāl bān-tee-la-dor')
fine — la multa (la mool'-ta)
front — delante (dā-lan'-tā)
fuel pump — la bomba de combustible (la bom'-ba dā kom-boos-tee'-blā)

garage — el garage (āl ga-ra^ᴸ-hā)
gasoline — la gasolina (la ga-so-lee^ᴸ-na)
to grease — engrasar (ān-gra-sar')
highway — la carretera (la ka-rrā-tā^ᴸ-ra)
ignition — el encendido (āl ān-sān-dee^ᴸ-do)
insurance — el seguro (āl sā-goo^ᴸ-ro)
left — izquierda (ees-kyār^ᴸ-da)
light — la luz (la loos)
mechanic — el mecánico (āl mā-ka^ᴸ-nee-ko)
muffler — el silenciador; el mofle (āl see-lān-see-ya-dor' āl mo^ᴸ-flā)
narrow — angosto; estrecho (an-gos^ᴸ-to; ās-trā^ᴸ-cho)
oil — el aceite (āl a-sā^ᴸ-tā)
to park — estacionar (ās-ta-syo-nar')
patrol — la patrulla (la pa-troo^ᴸ-ya)
pedestrian — el peatón (āl pā-ya-ton')
permit — el permiso (āl pār-mee^ᴸ-so)
piston — el pistón (āl pees-ton')
policeman — la presión (la prā-syon')
pump — la bomba (la bom^ᴸ-ba)
radiator — el radiador (āl ra-dya-dor')
right — derecha (dā-rā^ᴸ-cha)
rings — los anillos (los a-nee^ᴸ-yos)
river — el río (āl ree^ᴸ-yo)
road — el camino (āl ka-mee^ᴸ-no)
scooter — el escutér (āl ās-koo-tār')
signal light — la señal (la sān-yal')
to skid — patinar (pa-tee-nar')
spark plugs — las bujías (las boo-hee^ᴸ-yas)
speed limit — velocidad máxima (bā-lo-see-dad' mak^ᴸ-see-ma)
starter — el arranque (āl a-rran^ᴸ-kā)
steering wheel — el volante (āl bo-lan^ᴸ-tā)
telephone — el teléfono (āl tā-lā^ᴸ-fo-no)
tire — la llanta (la yan^ᴸ-ta)
to tow — remolcar (rā-mol-kar')
tow truck — la grúa (la groo^ᴸ-a)
traffic light — la luz del tránsito (la loos dāl tran^ᴸ-see-to)

transmission — la transmisión (la trans-mee-syon')
valve — la válvula (la bal'-boo-la)
wheel — la rueda (la rwā'-da)
wide — ancho (an'-cho)
windshield — el parabrisas (āl pa-ra-bree'-sas)
windshield wiper — el limpiaparabrisas (āl
  leem-pya-pa-ra-bree'-sas)

MEDICAL

I need a doctor. — Necesito un médico. (mā'-dee-ko)
I feel sick. — Me siento enfermo. (-a) (mā syān'-to
  ān-fār'-mo)
I have a stomach ache. — Tengo dolor de estómago.
  (ā-sto'-ma-go)
I have a headache. — Tengo dolor de cabeza.
I have a cold. — Tengo un resfriado. (rās-free-a'-do)
My throat hurts. — Me duele la garganta. (dwā'-lā)
_____
The definition and pronunciation of **all** words used will be
found in the Glossary.

I have a bad cough. — Tengo una tos formidable.
The bone is broken. — El hueso está roto. (wā'-so)
I feel dizzy. — Me siento mareado. (ma-rā-a'-do)
It hurts here. — Me duele aquí.
I have sprained my ankle. — Me he torcido el tobillo.
  (mā ā tor-see'-do āl to-bee'-yo)
I think I have food poisoning. — Creo que estoy
  intoxicado. (-a) (een-tok-see-ka'-do)
I have been vomiting. — He estado vomitando.
  (bo'-mee-tan'-do)
I have diarrhea. — Tengo diarrea. (dee-ya-rā'-a)
I can't sleep. — No puedo dormir. (dor-meer')
I'm expecting a baby. — Estoy encinta. (ān-seen'-ta)
I'm a diabetic. (epileptic) — Soy diabético. (-a)
  (epiléptico) (dee-a-bā'-tee-ko) (ā-pee-lāp'-tee-ko)

I'm allergic to aspirin. (penicillin) — Soy alérgico a la aspirina. (penicilina) (a-lär'-hee-ko)

I have a heart condition. — Sufro del corazón.

I have arthritis. — Tengo artritis. (ar-tree'-tees)

Can you give me a prescription? — ¿Puede usted darme una receta?

How many times a day should I take it? — ¿Cuántas veces al día debo tomarla? (bā'-säs)

Should I stay in bed? — ¿Guardo cama? (gwar'-do ka'-ma)

Is it serious? — ¿Es serio? (sā'-ryo)

Can I travel? — ¿Puedo viajar? (bya-har')

DENTIST

I need a dentist. — Necesito un dentista.

I have a toothache. — Tengo dolor de muelas. (do-lor' dā mwā'-las)

I've lost a filling. — He perdido un empaste.

Can you fix it temporarily? — ¿Puede arreglarlo temporalmente? (a-rrā-glar' lo tām-po-ral-mān'-tā)

I want novocaine, please. — Quiero novocaína, por favor. (no-bo-ca-ee'-na)

Can you fix my dentures? — ¿Puede arreglarme la dentadura postiza? (dän-ta-doo'-ra)

When will it be done? — ¿Cuándo estará hecha? (ā'-cha)

OPTICIAN

I broke my glasses. — Se me han roto las gafas.

When will they be ready? — ¿Cuándo estarán listas? (ās-ta-ran')

Can you change the lenses? — ¿Puede cambiar los lentes?

I want contact lenses. — Quiero lentes de contacto.

MEDICAL VOCABULARY

accident — el accidente (āl ak-see-dān'-tā)

allergic — alérgico (a-lär'-hee-ko)

ambulance — la ambulancia (la am-boo-lan'-see-ya)

appendicitis — la apendicitis (la a-pān-dee-see'-tees)

appointment — la cita (la see'-ta)

arm — el brazo (āl bra'-so)

aspirin — la aspirina (la a-spee-ree'-na)

back — la espalda (la ā-spal'-da)

bandage — la venda (la bān'-da)

bite — la picadura (la pee-ka-doo'-ra)

bone — el hueso (āl wā'-so)

broken — roto (ro'-to)

bruise — la contusión (la kon-too-syon')

burn — la quemadura (la kā-ma-doo'-ra)

cold (illness) — el resfriado (āl rās-free-a'-do)

contagious — contagioso (kon-ta-hee-o'-so)

cough — la tos (la tos)

cramp — el calambre (āl ka-lam'-brā)

cure — la cura; el remedio (la koo'-ra; āl rā-mā'-dyo)

cut — la cortadura (la kor-ta-doo'-ra)

dentist — el dentista (āl dān-tees'-ta)

diabetic — el diabético (āl dee-a-bā'-tee-ko)

diarrhea — la diarrea (la dee-ya-rā'-a)

dizzy — mareado (ma-r' -a'-do)

doctor — el doctor; el médico (āl dok-tor'

drugstore — la farmacia (la far-ma'-sya)

emergency — la emergencia; la urgencia (la
  ā-mar-hān'-sya; la oor-hān'-sya)

epileptic — epiléptico (ā-pee-lāp'-tee-ko)

eye — el ojo (āl o'-ho)

to faint — desmayarse (dās-may-yar'-sā)

fever — la fiebre (la fyā'-brā)

finger — el dedo (āl dā'-do)

flu — la gripe (la gree'-pā)

hand — la mano (la ma'-no)

hay fever — el catarro asmático (āl ka-ta'-rro
  as-ma'-tee-ko)

head — la cabeza (la ka-bā'-sa)

heart — el corazón (āl ko-ra-son')

hospital — el hospital (āl o-spee-tal')

indigestion — la indigestión (la een-dee-hās-tyon')
injection — la inyección (la een-yāk-syon')
leg — la pierna (la pyār'-na)
liver — el hígado (āl ee'-ga-do)
medicine — la medicina (la mā-dee-see'-na)
mouth — la boca (la bo'-ka)
nausea — el asco (āl as'-ko); la nausea (la naoo'-sā-a)
neck — el cuello (āl kwā'-yo)
nurse — la enfermera (la ān-fār-mā'-ra)
optician — el óptico (āl op'-tee-ko)
pain — el dolor (āl do-lor')
prescription — la receta (la rā-sā'-ta)
sick — enfermo (ān-fār'-mo)
skin — la piel (la pyāl)
sprain — la torcedura (la tor-sā-doo'-ra)
stomach — el estómago (āl ā-sto'-ma-go)
stomach ache — el dolor de estómago (āl do-lor' dā ā-sto'-ma-go)
sunburn — la quemadura del sol (la kā-mā-doo'-ra dāl sol)
sunstroke — la insolación (la een-so-la-syon')
temperature — la temperatura (la tām-pār-a-too'-ra)
throat — la garganta (la gar-gan'-ta)
tooth — el diente (āl dyān'-tā)
toothache — el dolor de muelas (āl do-lor' dā mwā'-las)
treatment — el tratamiento (āl tra-ta-myān'-to)
x-ray — rayos équis (ray'-yos ā-kees)

PHOTOGRAPHY

Is picture taking permitted? — ¿Se puede sacar fotos? (sā pwā'-dā sa-kar' fo'-tos)
What is the fee for taking pictures? — ¿Cuál es la tarifa por sacar fotos?
I would like film for this camera. — Quisiera película para esta cámara. (kee-syā'-ra-pā-lee'-koo-la)
I need two rolls of color film for slides. — Necesito dos

rollos de película en colores para diapositivas. (roy'-yos)
(dee-a-po-see-tee'-bas)

Do you have movie film? — ¿tiene película para cine?
(see'-nā)

I want this film developed, please. — Quiero revelar esta
película, por favor. (rā-bā-la'-do)

The definition and pronunciation of **all** words used will be
found in the Glossary.

I'd like two prints of each negative. — Quisiera dos
copias de cada negativo. (ko'-pyas) (nā-ga-tee'-bo)

May I take your picture? — ¿Me permite usted una foto?

When will it be ready? — ¿Cuándo estará?

My camera doesn't work. — Mi cámara no funciona.
(foon-syo'-na)

Can you fix it? — ¿Puede usted arreglarla? (a-rrā-glar'-la)

I can't rewind the film. — No puedo rebobinar la
película. (rā-bo-bee-nar')

The shutter won't close. — No se cierra el obturador.
(syā'-rra āl ob-too-ra-dor')

I'd like this enlarged. — Quisiera una ampliación de ésta.
(am-plee-a-cyon')

*Film is expensive in Latin America (except Panama). Bring
a good supply. A metal carrying strap is a good idea.*

PHOTOGRAPHY VOCABULARY

black and white — blanco y negro (blan'-ko ee nā'-gro)
camera — la cámara (la ka'-ma-ra)
color film — la película de colores (la pā-lee'-koo-la dā
ko-lo'-rās)
enlargement — la ampliación (la am-plee-a-syon')
develop — revelar (rā-bā-lar')
film — la película (la pā-lee'-koo-la)
filter — el filtro (āl feel'-tro)

flash bulb — la bombilla de flash (la bom-bee'-ya dā flash)
lens — el objetivo (āl ob-hā-tee'-bo); el lente (āl lān'-tā)
lens cap — la tapa del lente
light meter — el exposímetro (āl āks-po-see'-mā-tro)
movie film — la película de cine (la pā-lee'-koo-la dāl see'-nā)
negative — el negativo (āl nā-ga-tee'-bo)
photograph — la fotografía (la fo-to-gra-fee'-ya)
picture — la copia (la ko'-pya)
rangefinder — el telémetro (āl tā-lā'-mā-tro)
roll — el rollo (āl roy'-yo)
shutter — el obturador (āl ob-too-ra-dor')
slide — la diapositiva (la dee-a-po-see-tee'-ba)
snapshot — la instantánea (la een-stan-tan'-ā-ya)

CUSTOMS

Where do I go through customs? — ¿Dónde está la aduana? (a-dwa'-na)
Here is my passport. (vaccination certificate) — Aquí está mi pasaporte. (certificado de vacunación) (ba-koo-na-syon')
Do you have anything to declare? — ¿Tiene usted algo que declarar?
I have nothing to declare. — No tengo nada que declarar.
These are my bags. — Estas son mis maletas. (ma-lā'-tas)
I have a carton of cigarettes. — Tengo un cartón de cigarrillos. (see-ga-rree'-yos)
I have a bottle of whiskey. (wine) — Tengo una botella de whiskey. (vino) (botā'-ya dā wees'-kee)

The definition and pronunciation of **all** words used will be found in the Glossary.

It is for my personal use. — Es para mi uso personal. (oo'-so pār-so-nal')
I'm here on vacation. — Estoy aquí de vacaciones. (bā-ka-syo'-nās)

I'm here on business. — Estoy aquí de negocios.
  (nā-goʰ-syos)
These are gifts. — Estos son regalos.
Open this bag. — Abra esta maleta.
You'll have to pay duty on this. — Tendrá que pagar
  impuestos sobre ésto. (eem-pwāsʰ-tos)
Anything else? Nothing else. — Algo más? Nada maś.
You may go through now. — Ya puede pasar.

CUSTOMS VOCABULARY

alcohol — el alcohol (āl alʰ-ko-ol)
bag — la maleta (la ma-lāʰ-ta)
banknote — el billete de banco (āl bee-yāʰ-tā dā banʰ-ko)
bottle — la botella (la bo-tāʰ-ya)
box — la caja (la kaʰ-ha)
on business — de negocios (dā nā-goʰ-syos)
camera — la cámara (la kaʰ-ma-ra)
cigar — el puro (āl pooʰ-ro)
cigarettes — los cigarrillos (los see-ga-rreeʰ-yos)
to close — cerrar (sā-rrar')
customs — la aduana (la a-dwaʰ-na)
to declare — declarar (dā-kla-rar')
drugs — las drogas (las droʰ-gas)
duty — el impuesto (āl eem-pwāsʰ-to)
key — la llave (la yaʰ-bā)
label — la etiqueta (la ā-tee-kāʰ-ta)
luggage — el equipaje (āl ā-kee-paʰ-hā)
money — el dinero (āl dee-nāʰ-ro)
number — el número (āl nooʰ-mā-ro)
to open — abrir (a-breer')
passport — el pasaporte (āl pa-sa-porʰ-tā)
to pay — pagar (pa-gar')
porter — el mozo (āl moʰ-so)
present — el regalo (āl rā-gaʰ-lo)
suitcase — la maleta (la ma-lāʰ-ta)
tobacco — el tabaco (āl ta-baʰ-ko)

train — el tren (āl trãn)
traveler's check — el cheque de viajero (āl chã'-kā dā
  bya-hã'-ro)
trunk — el baúl (āl ba-ool')
on vacation — de vacaciones (dã ba-ka-syo'-nās)

EMERGENCIES

Help! — ¡Socorro! (so-ko'-rro)
Stop! — ¡Pare! (pa'-rā)
Hurry! — ¡De prisa! (dã pree'-sa)
Look out! — ¡Cuidado! (kwee-da'-do)
Fire! — ¡Incendio! (een-sãn'-dyo)
Leave me alone! — ¡Déjeme! (dã'-hā-mā)
Poison — Veneno (bā-nā'-no)
Police — Policía (po-lee-see'-ya)
Thief! — ¡Ladrón! (la-dron')
Don't worry — No se preocupe. (no sã prã-o'-koo-pā)
Don't move — No se mueva. (no sã mwã'-bā)

––––––––––

The definition and pronunciation of **all** words used will be
found in the Glossary.

SIGHTSEEING

I'd like to go sightseeing. — Quisiera ver los puntos de
  interés. (cen-tã-rās')
Is there a tourist office? — ¿Hay una oficina de turismo?
I'd like to see the city. — Quisiera ver la ciudad.
I want a map of the city. — Quiero un mapa de la ciudad.
Is there a sightseeing tour? — ¿Hay una excursión
  turística? (āks-koor-syon' too-rees'-tee-ka)
Where is the guide? — ¿Dónde está el guía? (gee'-ya)
Does he speak English? — ¿Habla inglés?
How long does the tour last? — ¿Cuánto tiempo dura la
  excursión?

What is the name of this place? — ¿Cómo se llama este lugar?

The definition and pronunciation of **all** words used will be found in the Glossary.

What is that building? — ¿Qué es ese edificio? (ā-dee-fee'-syo)

We want to go to the ruins. — Queremos ir a las ruinas. (rwee'-nas)

When was it built? — ¿Cuándo se construyó? (kon-stroo-yo')

I want to see the cathedral. — Quiero ver la catedral.

May we go in? — ¿Podemos entrar?

Is the museum open today? — ¿Está abierto el museo hoy?

May I take photographs? — ¿Se puede sacar fotos?

How much is the entrance fee? — ¿Cuánto cuesta la entrada?

The museums are closed today. — Los museos están cerrados hoy. (moo-sā'-os)

What is the name of that church? — ¿Cómo se llama esa iglesia? (ee-glā'-sya)

I want to see the art museum. — Quiero ver el museo de arte.

Is there a show on now? — ¿Hay una exposición ahora? (āks-po-see-syon')

Follow the guide. — Siga al guía. (gee'-ya)

Where is the main square? — ¿Dónde está la plaza principal? (preen-see-pal')

What is that monument? — ¿Qué es ese monumento?

We have walked a lot. — Hemos caminado mucho. (ā'-mos ka-mee-na'-do)

I'm tired. — Estoy cansado (-a).

Let's sit down a while. — Sentémonos un rato. (sān-tā'-mo-nos)

I'm looking for the market. — Busco el mercado.

Can you go on foot? — ¿Se puede ir a pie? (pee'-yā)

Is it far? — ¿Está lejos? (lāʟ-hos)

I am lost. — Estoy perdido. (pär-deeʟ-do)

Where is the zoo? — ¿Dónde está el zoológico? (so-o-loʟ-hee-ko)

We don't need a guide. — No necesitamos guía.

Which bus goes to the castle? — ¿Cuál autobús va al castillo? (kas-teeʟ-yo)

I'd like to go downtown. — Quisiera ir al centro.

What's the name of this river (lake) (volcano)? — ¿Cómo se llama este río (lago) (volcán)? (bol-kan')

I'd like to see the harbor. — Quisiera ver el puerto.

Which way to the beach? — ¿Por dónde está la playa?

We're interested in antiques. (archaeology) (folk arts). — Nos interesa las antigüedades. (la arqueología) (la artesanía). (an-tee-gwā-daʟ-dās) (ar-kā-o-lo-heeʟ-ya) (ar-tā-sa-neeʟ-ya)

Thank you for the tour. — Le agredezco la excursión.

I like it. — Me gusta.

I liked it. — Me gustó.

SIGHTSEEING VOCABULARY

admission — la entrada (la ān-traʟ-da)

altarpiece — el retablo (āl rā-tabʟ-lo)

avenue — la avenida (la a-bā-neeʟ-da)

bridge — el puente (āl pwānʟ-tā)

building — el edificio (āl ā-dee-feeʟ-syo)

castle — el castillo (āl kas-teeʟ-yo)

catacombs — las catacumbas (las ka-ta-koomʟ-bas)

cathedral — la catedral (la ka-tā-dral')

century — el siglo (āl seegʟ-lo)

chapel — la capilla (la ka-peeʟ-ya)

church — la iglesia (la ee-glāʟ-sya)

downtown — el centro (āl sānʟ-tro)

façade — la fachada (la fa-chaʟ-da)

fortress — la fortaleza (la for-ta-lāʟ-sa)

fountain — la fuente (la fwānʟ-tā)

gallery — la galería (la ga-lā-ree'-ya)

guide — el guía (al gee-ya); la guía (la gee-ya)

king — el rey (āl rā)

lake — el lago (āl la'-go)

map — el mapa (āl ma'-pa)

market — el mercado (āl mār-ka'-do)

monument — el monumento (āl mo-noo-mān'-to)

mountain — la montaña (la mon-tan'-ya)

museum — el museo (al moo-sā'-o)

painting — el cuadro (āl kwa'-dro)

palace — el palacio (āl pa-la'-syo)

park — el parque (āl par'-kā)

portrait — el retrato (āl rā-tra'-to)

pyramid — la pirámide (la pee-ra'-mee-dā)

queen — la reina (la rā'-ee-na)

ruins — las ruinas (las rwee'-nas)

sculpture — la escultura (la ās-kool-too'-ra)

square — la plaza (la pla'-sa)

street — la calle (la ka'-yā)

tomb — la tumba (la toom'-ba)

tour — la excursión (la āks-koor-syon')

tower — la torre (la t'-orrā)

university — la universidad (la oo-nee-bāar-see-dad')

zoo — el zoológico (āl so-o-lo'-kee-ko)

POST OFFICE

Where's the post office? — ¿Dónde está el correo? (ko-rrā'-o)

I want a stamp, please. — Quiero una estampilla, por favor. (ās-tam-pee'-ya)

How much does it cost to send this package? — ¿Cuánto cuesta mandar este paquete? (pa-kā'-tā)

I want to send it airmail. — Quiero mandarlo por aéreo. (a-ā'-rā-o)

How much is the postage to New York? — ¿Cuál es el franqueo a Nueva York? (fran-kā'-o)

Can I insure this package? — ¿Puedo asegurar este paquete? (a-sā-goo-rar')

When does the post office open? (close) — ¿A qué hora se abre (cierra) el correo?

The definition and pronunciation of **all** words used will be found in the Glossary.

Where is the mailbox? — ¿Dónde está el buzón? (boo-sonʹ)

Are there any letters for me? — ¿Hay algunas cartas para mí?

My name is . . . — Me llamo . . . (ya'-mo)

I want to cash a postal money order. — Quiero cambiar un giro. (hee'-ro)

Where is the general delivery section? — ¿Dónde está la lista de correos?

I want to send a telegram. — Quiero mandar un telegrama. (tāa lā gra'-ma)

How much is it per word? — ¿Cuánto cuesta por palabra?

I want to send this special delivery. — Quiero mandar éste por entrega inmediata. (ān-trā'-ga een-mā-dya'-ta)

How long will it take? — ¿Cuánto tardará?

Hint: To receive General Delivery mail, have it addressed to your first and last name, Lista de Correos, the city, the state, and the country. Bring your identification. If there is more than one post office, go to the main branch (correo central) *and ask for the* Lista de Correos.

POST OFFICE VOCABULARY

address — la dirección (la dee-rāk-syonʹ)
airmail — el correo aéreo (āl ko-rrā'-o a-ā'-rā-o)
cablegram — el cablegrama (āl ka-blā-gra'-ma)

customs declaration — la declaración para la aduana (la dā-kla-ra-syon' pa'-ra la a-dua'-na)

delivery — la entrega (la āan-trā'-ga)

express — urgente (orr-hāan'-tā)

general delivery — la lista de correos (la lees'-ta dā ·ko-rrā'-os)

to insure — asegurar (a-sā-goo-rar')

letter — la carta (la kar'-ta)

mail — el correo (āl ko-rrā'-o)

mailbox — el buzón (āl boo-son')

mailman — el cartero (āl kar-tā'-ro)

money order — el giro postal (āl hee'-ro pos-tal')

package — el paquete (āl pa-kā'-tā)

postage — el franqueo (āl fran-kā'-o)

postcard — la tarjeta postal (la tar-hā'-ta pos-tal')

post office — el correo (al ko-rrā'-o)

to register — certificar (sār-tee-fee-kar')

regular mail — el correo ordinario (al ko-rrā'-o or-dee-na'-ryo)

to send — mandar (man-dar')

to sign — firmar (feer-mar')

special delivery — la entrega inmediata (la ān-trā'-ga een-mā-dya'-ta)

stamp — la estampilla (la āas-tam-pee'-ya); el sello (āl sā'-yo)

telegram — el telegrama (āl tā-lā-gra'-ma)

TRANSPORTATION

PLANE

I want to go to the airport. — Quiero ir al aeropuerto. (a-ā-ro-pwār'-to)

Is there limousine service to the airport? — ¿Hay servicio de transportación al aeropuerto? (trans-por-ta-syon')

I'd like two tickets to ... — Quisiera dos boletos a ...

Is it a nonstop flight? — ¿Es un vuelo sin escalas?
(bwā'-lo seen ās-ka'-las)

What time does the plane leave? — ¿A qué hora sale el
avión? (a-byon')

What time does it arrive? — ¿A qué hora llega?

From which gate? — ¿De cuál puerta?

That flight is filled. — Ese vuelo está completo.

When does the next flight leave? — ¿Cuándo sale el
próximo vuelo?

────────

The definition and pronunciation of **all** words used will be
found in the Glossary.

When must I check in? — ¿A qué hora hay que estar en la
terminal?

I'd like to confirm my reservation. — Quisiera confirmar
mi reservación. (rā-sār-ba-syon')

Can I change my seat? — ¿Puedo cambiar mi asiento?
(a-syān'-to)

I would like a pillow (magazine) (more coffee), please.
— Quisiera una almohada (una revista) (más cafe), por
favor. (al-mo-a'-da)

What city are we flying over? — ¿Sobre qué cuidad
estamos volando? (syoo-dad')

I'm feeling sick. — Estoy mareado.

Where is the bathroom? — ¿Dónde está el servicio? (el
baño)

Please fasten your seat belts. — Fijen los cinturones, por
favor. (fee'-hān) (seen-too-ro'-nās)

The plane is landing. (is taking off) — El avión aterriza.
(despega) (a-tā-rree'-sa)

There will be a delay. — Habrá una demora. (a-bra')
(dā-mo'-ra)

We have arrived. — Hemos llegado. (ā'-mos yā-ga'-do)

TRAIN

I want to go to the railroad station. — Quiero ir a la
estación de ferrocarril. (fā-rro-ka-rreel')

I'd like a first class ticket to . . . — Quisiera un boleto de
primera clase a . . .

One way. Round trip. — De ida. De ida y vuelta. (ee-da
ee bwāl-ta)

I need a porter. — Necesito un mozo.

These are my bags. — Estas son mis maletas. (ma-lā-tas)

What's the fare? — ¿Cuál es la tarifa? (kwal) (ta-ree-fa)

I want a sleeper. — Quiero una cama.

Is there a dining car? — ¿Hay un carro comedor? (ka-rro
ko-mā-dor')

What time does the train leave? — ¿A qué hora sale el
tren?

How long does it take? — ¿Cuánto tarda?

Is this seat occupied? — ¿Está ocupado este asiento?
(a-syān-to)

It's taken. — Está ocupado.

I want a private compartment. — Quiero un
compartimiento particular. (kom-par-tee-myān-to
par-tee-koo-lar')

Where is the bathroom? — ¿Dónde está el baño?

How long does the train stop here? — ¿Cuánto tiempo
para el tren aquí?

**I want to pick up my luggage. Quiero recoger mi
equipaje.** (rā-ko-hār') (ā-kee-pa-hā)

BOAT

Is there a boat from here to . . . ? — ¿Hay un barco de
aquí a . . . ?

Where is the pier? — ¿Dónde está el muelle? (mwā-yā)

I want a first (second) class cabin. (berth) — Quiero un
camarote de primera (segunda) clase. (litera)
(ka-maro-tā) (lee-tā-ra)

When does the ship leave? — ¿Cuándo sale el buque?
(boo-kā)

I'm looking for the dining room. — Busco el comedor.

**I would like a deck chair. Quisiera una silla de
cubierta.** (see-ya dā koo-byār-ta)

I would like to eat by the swimming pool. — Quisiera comer cerca de la piscina. (pee-see'-na)

Where are the life preservers? — ¿Dónde están los salvavidas? (sal-ba-bee'-das)

I am seasick. — Estoy mareado. (ma-rā-a'-do)

When do we arrive? — ¿Cuándo llegamos? (yā-ga'-mos)

Where do we pick up our luggage? — ¿Dónde recogemos el equipaje? (rā-ko-hā'-mos)

TRANSPORTATION VOCABULARY

airplane — el avión (āl a-byón)

airport — el aeropuerto (āl a-ā-ro-pwār'-to)

airsick — mareado (ma-rā-a'-do)

arrival — la llegada (la yā-ga'-da)

to arrive — llegar (yā-gar')

ashtray — el cenicero (āl sā-nee-sā'-ro)

berth — la litera (la lee-tā'-ra)

boat — el barco (āl bar'-ko)

cabin — el camarote (āl ka-ma-ro'-tā)

car — el coche (āl ko'-chā)

cloud — la nube (la noo'-bā)

compartment — el compartimiento (āl kom-par-tee-myān'-to)

corner — el rincón (āl rreen-kon')

corridor — el pasillo (āl pa-see'-yo)

crew — la tripulación (la tree-poo-la syón)

crossing — la travesía (la tra-bā-see'-ya)

deck — la cubierta (la koo-byār'-ta)

deck chair — la silla de cubierta (la see'-ya dā koo-byār'-ta)

delay — la demora (la dā-mo'-ra)

departure — la salida (la sa-lee'-da)

dining car — el carro comedor (āl ka'-rro ko-mā-dor')

to disembark — desembarcar (dās-ām-bar-kar')

dock — el muelle (āl mwā'-yā)

emergency cord — el timbre de alarma (āl teem'-brā dā a-lar'-ma)

engine — la máquina (la ma'-kee-na); el motor (āl mo-tor')

entrance — la entrada (la ān-tra'-da)

exit — la salida (la sa-lee'-da)

first class — primera clase (pree-mā'-ra kla'-sā)

flight — el vuelo (āl bwā'-lo)

gate — la puerta (la pwār'-ta)

harbour — el puerto (āl pwār'-to)

ladder — el escalera (la ās-ka-lā'-ra)

to land — aterrizar (a-tā-rree-sar')

life preserver — el salvavidas (āl sal-ba-bee'-das)

luggage — el equipaje (āl ā-kee-pa'-hā)

luggage ticket — el talón (āl ta-lon')

next — próximo (prok'-see-mo)

occupied — ocupado (o-koo-pa'-do)

passenger — el pasajero (āl pa-sa-hā'-ro)

to pick up — recoger (rā-ko-hār')

pier — el muelle (āl mwā'-yā)

pillow — la almohada (la al-mo-a'-da)

pilot — el piloto (āl pee-lo'-to)

place — el sitio (āl see'-tyo); el lugar (āl loo-gar')

plane — el avión (āl a-byon')

platform — el andén (āl andān')

port — el puerto (āl pwār'-to)

porter — el mozo (āl mo'-so)

railroad — el ferrocarril (āl fā-rro-ka-rreel')

runway — la pista (la pees'-ta)

safety belt — el cinturón de seguridad (āl seen-too-ron' dā sā-goo-ree-dad')

seat — el asiento (āl a-syān'-to)

second class — segunda clase (sā-goon'-da kla'-sā)

sick — mareado (ma-rā-a'-do)

sleeping car — el coche-camas (āl ko'-chā ka'-mas)

to smoke — fumar (foo-mar')

smokers — los fumadores (los foo-ma-do'-rās)

station — la estación (la ās-ta-syon')

stewardess — la azafata (la a-sa-fa'-ta); la camarera de avión (la ka-ma-rã'-ra dã a-byon')

to stop — parar (pa-rar')

suitcase — la maleta (la ma-lã'-ta)

swimming pool — la piscina (la pee-see'-na)

to take off — despegar (dãs-pã-gar')

ticket — el boleto (ãl bo-lã'-to)

timetable — el horario (ãl o-ra'-ree-o)

train — el tren (ãl trãn)

vacant — libre (lee'-brã)

valid — válido (ba'-lee-do)

waiting room — la sala de espera (la sa'-la dã ãs-pã'-ra)

window — la ventanilla (la bãn-ta-nee'-ya)

wing — el ala (el a'-la)

GLOSSARY

a — un (oon); una (oo⌐-na)
abalone — el abulón (āl a-boo-lo⌐-n)
(to be) able — poder (po-d⌐-ar)
aboard — a bordo (a bor⌐-do)
about — acerca de (a-sār⌐-ka dā)
above — arriba (arree⌐-ba)
absolutely — absolutamente (ab-so-loo-ta-mān⌐-tā)
accelerator — el acelerador (āl ak-sāl-ā-ra-dor')
accent — el acento (āl a-sān⌐-to)
to accept — aceptar (a-sāp-tar')
accident — el accidente (āl ak-see-dān⌐-tā)
according to — según (sā-goon')
account — la cuenta (la kwān⌐-ta)
across — a través de (a tra-bās' dā)
actor — el actor (āl ak-tor')
actress — la actriz (la ak-trees')
actual — verdadero (bār-da-dā⌐-ro)
to add — añadir (an-ya-deer'); sumar (soo-mar')
address — la dirección (la dee-rāk-syon')
to admire — admirar (ad-mee-rar')
admission — la entrada (la ān-tra⌐-da)
to advance — avanzar (a-ban-sar')
advantage — la ventaja (la bān-ta⌐-ha)
advertisement — el anuncio (āl a-noon⌐-syo)
advice — el consejo (āl kon-sā⌐-ho)
(to be) afraid — tener miedo (tā-nār⌐- myā⌐-do); temer (tā-mār')
after — después de (dās-pwās')
afternoon — la tarde (la tar-da)
afterwards — después (das pwas)
age — la edad (la ā-dad')

62

again — otra vez (oᴸ-tra bās)

against — contra (konᴸ-tra)

agency — la agencia (la a-hānᴸ-sya)

agent — el agente (āl a-hānᴸ-tā)

ago — hace (aᴸ-sā)

to agree — estar de acuredo (ās-tarᴸ-dā a-kwārᴸ-do)

agreeable — agradable (a-gra-daᴸ-blā)

air — el aire (āl ayᴸ-rā)

air conditioned — aire acondicionado (ayᴸ-rā a-kon-dee-syo-naᴸ-do)

airline — la línea aerea (la leeᴸ-nā-ya a-āᴸ-rā-a)

airmail — correo aereo (ko-rrāᴸ-o a-āᴸ-rā-o)

airplane — el avión (āl a-ā-ro-pwārᴸ-to)

airsick — mareado (ma-rā-aᴸ-do)

a la carte — a la carta (a la karᴸ-ta)

alarm — la alarma (la a-larᴸ-ma)

alarm clock — el despertador (āl dās-pār-ta-dorʼ)

alcohol — el alcohol (āl al-ko-olʼ)

alike — semejante (sā-mā-hanᴸ-tā)

alive — vivo (beeᴸ-bo)

all — todo (toᴸ-do)

allergic — alérgico (a-lārᴸ-hee-ko)

to allow — permitir (pār-mee-teerʼ)

all right — bueno (bwāᴸ-no); está bien (ās-taʼ byān)

almond — la almendra (la al-mānᴸ-dra)

almost — casi (kaᴸ-see)

alone — solo (soᴸ-lo)

along — a lo largo (a lo larᴸ-go)

already — ya (ya)

alright — está bien (ās-taʼ byān)

also — también (tam-byānʼ)

altar — el altar (āl al-tarʼ)

altarpiece — el retablo (āl rā-tabᴸ-lo)

although — aunque (aoonᴸ-kā)

always — siempre (syāmᴸ-prā)

(I) am — soy (soy); estoy (ās-toyʼ)

ambassador — el embajador (āl ām-ba-ha-dorʼ)

ambulance — la ambulancia (la am-boo-lanᴸ-see-ya)

American — el americano (āl a-mā-ree-ka¹-no)

among — entre (ān¹-trā)

amount — la cantidad (la kan-tee-dad¹)

to amuse — divertir (dee-bār-teer¹)

an — un (oon); una (oo¹-na)

anchovy — la anchoa (la an-cho¹-a)

and — y (ee)

angry — enojado (ā-no-ha¹-do)

animal — el animal (āl a-nee-mal¹)

ankle — el tobillo (āl to-bee¹-yo)

to announce — anunciar (a-noon-syar¹)

to annoy — molestar (mo-lās-tar¹)

another — otro (o¹-tro)

answer — la respuesta (la rās-pwās¹-ta)

to answer — contestar (kon-tās-tar¹)

antique — antiguo (an-tee¹-gwo)

antiques — las antigüedades (las an-tee-gwā-da¹-dās)

anxious — ansioso (an-syo¹-so)

any — alguno (ai-goo¹-no)

anyone — alguien (al¹-gyān)

anything — algo (al¹-go); cualquier cosa (kwal-kyār¹ ko¹-sa)

anyway — de todos modos (dā to¹-dos mo¹-dos)

anywhere — dondequiera (don-dā-kyā¹-ra)

apartment — el apartamiento (āl a-par-ta-myān¹-to)

to apologize — excusar (āks-koo-sar¹); disculparse
(dees-kool-par¹-sā)

to appear — aparecer (a-pa-rā-sār¹)

appendicitis — la apendicitis (la a-pān-dee-see¹-tees)

appendix — el apéndice (āl a-pān¹-dee-sā)

appetite — el apetito (āl a-pā-tee¹-to)

appetizer — el entremés (āl ān-trā-mās¹); el aperitivo (āl
a-pā-ree-tee¹-bo)

apple — la manzana (la man-sa¹-na)

appointment — la cita (la see¹-ta)

to appreciate — apreciar (a-prā-syar¹)

to approve — aprobar (a-pro-bar¹)

approximately — aproximadamente
(a-prok-see-ma-da-mān¹-tā)

apricot — el albaricoque (āl al-ba-ree-ko'-kā); el chabacano (āl cha-ba-ka'-no)

April — abril (a-breel')

arch — el arco (āl ar'-ko)

archaeology — la arqueología (la ar-lā-o-lo-hee'-ya)

architect — el arquitecto (ā; ar-kee-tāk'-to)

architecture — la arquitectura (la ar-kee-tāk-too'-ra)

to argue — disputar (dees-poo-tar')

arm — el brazo (āl bra'-so)

around — alrededor (al-rā-dā-dor')

to arrange — arreglar (a-rrā-glar')

to arrest — arestar (a-ɪās-tar')

arrival — la llegada (la yā-ga'-da)

to arrive — llegar (yā-gar')

art — el arte (āl ar'-tā)

art gallery — la galería de arte (la ga-lā-ree'-ya dā ar'-tā)

arthritis — la artritis (la ar-tree'-tees)

artichoke — la alcachofa (la al-ka-cho'-fa)

article — el artículo (āl artee'-koo-lo)

artificial — artificial (ar-tee-fee-syal')

artist — el artista (āl ar-tees'-ta)

as — como (ko'-mo)

as much as — tanto como (tan'-to ko'-mo)

as well — también (tam-byān')

ashamed — avergonzado (a-bār-gon-sa'-do)

ashore — en tierra (ān tyā'-rra)

ashtray — el cenicero (āl sā-nee-sā'-ro)

to ask — preguntar (prā-goon-tar')

to ask for — pedir (pā-deer')

asleep — dormido (dor-mee'-do)

asparagus — el espárrago (āl ās-pa'-rra-go)

aspirin — la aspirina (la as-pee-ree'-na)

to assist — ayudar (a-yoo-dar')

assistant — el asistente (āl a-sees-tān'-tā)

to assure — asegurar (a-sā-goo-rar')

at — a (a); en (ān)

at last — al fin (al feen)

Atlantic — Atlántico (at-lan'-tee-ko)

at once — en seguida (ān sā-gee⁴-da)
atmosphere — el ambiente (āl am-byān⁴-tā)
to attempt — probar (pro-bar')
to attend — asistir a (a-sees-teer' a)
attention — la atención (la a-tān-syon')
to attract — atraer (a-tra-yār')
audience — el público (āl poo⁴-blee-ko)
August — agosto (a-gos⁴-to)
aunt — la tía (la tee⁴-ya)
author — el autor (āl aoo-tor')
authority — la autoridad (la aoo-to-ree-dad')
automobile — el automóvil (āl aoo-to-mo⁴-beel)
autumn — el otoño (āl-ton⁴-yo)
available — disponible (dee-po-nee⁴-blā)
avenue — la avenida (la a-bā-nee⁴-blā)
to avoid — evitar (ā-bee-tar')
to await — esperar (ās-pā-rar')
awake — despierto (dās-pyār⁴-to)
away — fuera (fwā⁴-ra)
axle — el eje (āl ā⁴-hā)
baby — el bebé (āl bā-bā'); el nene (āl nā⁴-nā)
bachelor — el soltero (āl sol-tā⁴-ro)
back (direction) — detrás (dā-tras')
back — la espalda (la ās-pal⁴-da)
bacon — el tocino (āl to-see⁴-no)
bad — malo (ma⁴-lo)
bag — la maleta (la ma-lā⁴-ta); la bolsa (la bol⁴-sa)
baggage — el equipaje (āl ā-kee-pa⁴-hā)
baggage check — el talón (āl ta-lon')
to bake — hornear (or-nā-yar')
bakery — la panadería (la pa-na-dā-ree⁴-ya)
balcony — el balcón (āl bal-kon')
ball (dance) — el baile (āl bay⁴-lā)
ball — la pelota (la pā-lo⁴-ta)
banana — el plátano (āl pla⁴-ta-no)
band — la banda (la ban⁴-da)
bandage — la venda (la bān⁴-da)
bandaid — la bandita (la ban-dee⁴-ta)

bank — el banco (āl banʼ-ko)

banknote — el billete de banco (āl bee-yāʼ-tā dā banʼ-ko)

bar — el bar (āl bar)

barbecue — la barbacoa (la bar-ba-koʼ-a)

barber shop — la peluquería (la pā-loo-kā-reeʼ-ya)

bargain — la ganga (la ganʼ-ga)

basket — la cesta (la sāsʼ-ta); la canasta (la ka-nasʼ-ta)

bath — el baño (āl banʼ-yo)

to bathe — bañarse (ban-yarʼ-sā)

bathing suit — el traje de baño (āl tra-hā dā banʼ-yo)

bathroom — el baño (āl banʼ-yo)

battery — la batería (la ba-tā-reeʼ-ya)

bay — la bahía (la ba-eeʼ-ya)

to be — estar (ās-tarʼ); ser (sār)

beach — la playa (la plaʼ-ya)

bean — el frijol (āl free-holʼ)

beard — la barba (la barʼ-ba)

beautiful — bonito (bo-neeʼ-to); bello (bāʼ-yo); lindo (leenʼ-do)

beauty parlor — el salón de belleza (āl sa-lonʼdā bā-yāʼ-sa)

because — porque (por-kāʼ)

bed — la cama (la kaʼ-ma)

bedroom — el dormitorio (āl dor-mee-to-ʼree-o)

bee — la abeja (la a-bāʼ-ha)

beef — la res (la rās)

beef steak — el bistec (āl beesʼtāk)

beer — la cerveza (la sār-bāʼsa)

beet — el betabel (āl bā-ta-bālʼ)

before — antes de (anʼtās dā)

to begin — empezar (ām-pā-sarʼ)

beginning — el principio (āl preen-seeʼpyo)

behind — detrás de (dā-trasʼ dā)

to believe — creer (krā-yārʼ)

bell — el timbre (āl teemʼ-brā)l la campana (la kam-paʼ-na)

to belong to — pertenecer (pār-tā-nā-sārʼ)

below — debajo de (dā-baʼ-ho dā)

belt — el cinto (āl seen'-to)

berth — la litera (la lee-tā'-ra)

beside — al lado de (al la'-do dā)

besides — además (a-dā-mas')

best — lo mejor (lo mā-hor')

better — mejor (mā-hor')

between — entre (ān'-trā)

beverage — la bebida (la bā-bee'-da)

bicycle — la bicicleta (la bee-see-klā'-ta)

big — grande (gran'-dā)

bill — el billete (āl bee-yā'-tā); la cuenta (la kwān'-ta)

bird — el ave (āl a'-bā); el pájaro (āl pa-ha-ro)

birthday — el cumpleaños (āl koom-plā-an'-yos)

a bit — un poquito (oon po-kee'-to)

bite — la picadura (la pee-ka-doo'-ra)

to bite — morder (mor-dār')

black — negro (nā'-gro)

black and white — blanco y negro (blan'-ko ee nā'-gro)

blanket — la cobija (la ko-bee'-ha)

to bleed — sangrar (san-grar')

blind — ciego (syā'-go)

blister — la ampolla (la am-poy'-ya)

blond — rubio (roo'-byo)

blood — la sangre (la san'-grā)

blouse — la blusa (la bloo'-sa)

blue — azul (a-sool')

boarding house — la pensión (la pān-syon'); la casa de huéspedes (la ka'-sa dā sās'-pā-dās)

boat — el barco (āl bar'-ko)

body — el cuerpo (āl kwār'-po)

to boil — hervir (ār-beer')

bone — el hueso (āl wā'-so)

book — el libro (āl lee'-bro)

bookstore — la librería (la lee-brā-ree'-ya)

boot — la bota (la bo'-ta)

border — la frontera (la fron-tā'-ra)

(to be) born — nacer (na-sār')

68

to borrow — prestar (präs-tar'); pedir prestado (pä-deer' präs-ta'-do)

both — ambos (am'-bos)

to bother — molestar (mo-läs-tar')

bottle — la botella (la bo-tä'-ya)

bottom — el fondo (äl fon'-do)

box — la caja (la k'-ha)

boy — el muchacho (äl moo-cha'-cho)

bracelet — la pulsera (la pool-sä'-ra)

brain — el seso (äl sä'-so)

to brake — los frenos (los frä'-nos)

brandy — el coñac (äl kon'-yak)

brassiere — el sostén (äl sos-tän')

brave — valiente (bal-yän'-tä)

bread — el pan (äl pan)

breaded steak — la milanesa (la mee-la-nä'-sa)

to break — romper (rom-pär')

to break down — estropearse (äs-tro-pä-yar'-sä)

breakfast — el desayuno (äl däs-ay-yoo'-no)

breast — la pechuga (of a bird) (la pä-choo'-ga); el pecho (äl pä'-cho)

to breathe — respirar (räs-pee-rar')

bridge — el puente (äl pwän'-tä)

bright — claro (kla'-ro)

to bring — traer (tra-yär')

British — británico (bree-t'-nee-ko)

broken — roto (ro'-to); quebrado (kä-bra'-do)

brooch — el broche (äl bro'-chä)

broth — el caldo (äl kal'-do)

brother — el hermano (äl är-ma'-no)

brown — moreno (mo-rä'-no); café (ka-fä'); pardo (par'-do); marron (ma-rron')

bruise — la contusión (la kon-too-syon')

brunette — moreno (mo-rä'-no)

brush — el cepillo (äl sä-pee'-yo)

to brush — cepillar (sä-pee-yar')

bucket — el cubo (äl koo'-bo); el balde (äl bal'-dä)

to build — construir (kon-stroo-eer')

building — el edificio (āl ā-dee-fee'-syo)

bull — el toro (āl to'-ro)

bullfight — la corrida de toros (la ko-rree'-da dā to'-ros)

burn — la quemadura (la kā-ma-doo'-ra)

to burn — quemar (kā-mar')

to burst — reventar (rā-bān-tar')

bus — el autobús (āl aoo-to-boos'); el camión (āl ka-myon')

bus stop — la parada de autobuses (la pa-ra'-da dā aoo-to-boo'-sās)

business — el negocio (āl nā-go'-syo)

busy — ocupado (o-koo-pa'-do)

but — pero (pā-ro)

butcher shop — la carnicería (la kar-nee-sā-ree'-ya)

butter — la mantequilla (la man-tā-kee'-ya)

button — el botón (āl bot-ton')

to buy — comprar (kom-prar')

by — por (por); cerca de (sār'-ka dā)

cabbage — la col (la kol)

cabin — el camarote (on ship) (āl ka-ma-ro'-tā); la babaña (la ka-ban'-ya); la choza (la cho'-sa)

cablegram — el cablegrama (āl ka-blā-gra'-ma)

cafe — el café (āl ka-fā')

cake — el pastel (āl pas-tāl')

call — la llamada (la ya-ma'-da)

to call — llamar (ya-mar')

camera — la cámera (la ka'-ma-ra)

to camp — acampar (a-kam-par')

can (to be able) — poder (po-dār')

Canadian — el canadiense (āl ka-na-dyān'-sā)

canal — el canal (āl ka-nal')

to cancel — cancelar (kan-sā-lar')

candy — los dulces (los dool'-sās)

candy store — la dulcería (la dool-sā-ree'-ya)

canoe — la canoa (la ka-no'-a)

cap — la gorra (la go'-rra)

capital — la capital (la ka-pee-tal')

car — el coche (āl ko'-chā); el automóvil (āl aoo-to-m'-beel); el carro (āl ka'-rro)

carat — el quilate (āl kee-la'-tā)

carburetor — el carburador (āl kar-boo-ra-dor')

card — la tarjeta (la tar-hā'-ta)

cardboard — el cartón (āl kar-ton')

care — el cuidado (āl kwee-da'-do)

careful — cuidadoso (kwee-da-do'-so)

carpet — la alfombra (la al-fom'-bra)

carrot — la zanahoria (la sa-na-o'-ree-a)

to carry — llevar (yā-bar')

carton — el cartón (āl kar-ton')

cash — al contado (al kon-ta'-do)

to cash — cambiar (kam-byar'); cobrar (ko-brar')

cashier — el cajero (āl ka-hā'-ro)

cashier's window — la caja (la ka'-ha); pagos (pa'-gos)

castle — el castillo (āl kas-tee'-yo)

cat — el gato (āl ga'-to)

catacombs — las catacumbas (las ka-ta-koom'-bas)

catalogue — el catálogo (āl ka-ta'-lo-go)

to catch — coger (ko-hār')

cathedral — la catedral (la ka-tā-dral')

Catholic — católico (ka-to'-lee-ko)

catsup — la salsa de tomate (la sal'-sa dā to-ma'-tā)

cattle — el ganado (āl ga-na'-do)

cauliflower — la coliflor (la ko-lee-flor')

caution — cuidado (kwee-da'-do); precaución (prā-kaoo-syon')

cave — la cueva (la kwā'-ba)

ceiling — el techo (āl tā'-cho)

celery — el apio (āl a'-pyo)

cellar — el sótano (āl so'-ta-no)

cemetery — el cemeterio (āl sā-mān-tā'-ree-yo)

century — el centímetro (āl sān-tee'-mā-tro)

century — el siglo (āl seeg'-lo)

ceremony — la ceremonia (la sā-rā-mo-nee'-ya)

certain — cierto (syār'-to)

certificate — la certificación (la sār-tee-fee-ka-syon')

chair — la silla (la see⌐-ya)

chambermaid — la camarera (la ka-ma-rā⌐-ya)

champagne — la champaña (la cham-pan⌐-ya)

chance — la oportunidad (la o-por-too-nee-dad')

change (silver) — el cambio (āl kam⌐-byo); el suelto (āl swāl⌐-to); el menudo (āl mā-noo⌐-do)

to change — cambiar (kam-byar')

chapel — la capilla (la ka-pee⌐-ya)

to charge — cobrar (ko-brar')

charming — encantador (ān-kan-ta-dor')

cheap — barato (ba-ra⌐-to)

check — el cheque (āl chā⌐-kā); la cuenta (la kwān⌐-ta)

to check — revisar (rā-bee-sar')

cheek — la mejilla (la mā-hee⌐-ya)

cheese — el queso (āl kā⌐-so)

cherry — la cereza (la sā-rā⌐-sa)

chest — el pecho (āl pā⌐-cho)

chestnut — la castaña (la kas-tan⌐-ya)

chicken — el pollo (āl poy⌐-yo)

child — el niño (āl neen⌐-yo)

chin — la barba (la bar⌐-ba)

china — la porcelana (la por-sā-la⌐-na)

Chinese — chino (chee⌐-no)

chocolate — el chocolate (āl cho-ko-lā⌐-tā)

to choose — escoger (ās-ko-hā4')

chop — la chuleta (la choo-lā⌐-ta)

Christmas — la Navidad (la na-bee-dad')

church — la iglesia (la ee-glā⌐-sya)

cider — la sidra (la see⌐-dra)

cigar — el puro (āl poo⌐-ro)

cigarette — el cigarro (āl see-ga⌐-rro); el cigarillo (āl see-gar-rre⌐-yo)

cigarette lighter — el encendedor (āl ān-sān-dā-dor')

circle — el círculo (āl seer⌐-koo-lo)

citizen — el ciudadano (āl syoo-da-da⌐-no)

city — la ciudad (la syoo-dad')

clam — la almeja (la al-mā⌐-ha)

class — la calse (la kla⌐-sā)

to classify — clasificar (kla-see-fee-kar')
clean — limpio (leem'-pyo)
to clean — limpiar (leem-pyar')
cleaner's — la tintorería (la teen-to-rā-ree'-ya)
clear — claro (kla'-ro)
clock — el reloj (āl rā'-loh)
close — cerca (sār'-ka)
to close — cerrar (sā-rrar')
closed — cerrado (sā-rra'-do)
closet — el armario (āal ar-ma'-ryo)
cloth — la tela (la tā'-la)
clothes — la ropa (la ro'-pa)
cloud — la nube (la noo'-bā)
clutch — el embrague (āl ām-bra'-gā)
coast — la costa (la kos'-ta)
coat — el abrigo (āl a-bree'-go)
cock — el gallo (āl gay'-yo)
cockfight — la pelea de gallos (la pā-lā'-a dā gay'-yos)
cocktail — el coctel (āl kok-tāl')
coconut — el coco (āl ko'-ko)
coffee — el café (āl ka-fā')
cognac — el coñac (āl kon-yak')
coin — la moneda (la mo-nā'-da)
cold (sickness) — el resfriado (āl rās-free-a'-do)
cold — frío (free'-yo)
to be cold — tener frío (tā-nār'- free'--yo)
cold cuts — los fiambres (los fyam'-brās)
collection — la colección (la ko-lāk-syon')
to collide — chocar (cho-kar')
color — el color (āl ko-lor')
color film — la película (la pā-lee'-koo-la)
comb — el peine (āl pā'-nā)
to comb — peinar (pā-nar')
to come — venir (bā-neer')
come in — adelante (a-dā-lan'-tā); pase (pa'-sā)
comfortable — cómodo (ko'-mo-do)
company — la compañía (la kom-pan'-ya)
compartment — el compartimiento (āl kom-par-tee-myān'-to)

to complain — quejarse (kā-har'-sā)

complete — completo (kom-plā'-to)

compliment — el cumplido (āl kom-plee'-do)

concert — el concierto (āl kon-syār-to)

condition — la condición (la kon-dee-syon')

conductor — el cobrador (āl ko-bra-dor')

to confirm — confirmar (kon-feer-mar')

to confuse — confundir (kon-foon-deer')

congratulations — felicidades (fā-lee-see-da'-dās)

to connect — conectar (ko-nāk-tar')

to consider — considerar (kon-see-dāa-rar')

to construct — construir (kon-stroo-eer')

consul — el cónsul (āl kon'-sool)

consulate — el consulado (āl kon-soo-la'-do)

contact lenses — los lentes de contacto (los lān'-tās dā kon-tak'-to)

contagious — contagioso (kon-ta-hee-o'-so)

to contain — contener (kon-tā-nār')

contented — contento (kon-tān'-to)

contraceptives — los contraceptivos (los kon-tra-sāp-tee'-bos)

convent — el convento (āl kon-bān'-to)

conversation — la conversación (la kon-bār-sa-syon')

convenient — conveniente (kon-bān-yān'-tā)

cook — el cocinero (āl ko-see-nā'-ro)

to cook — cocer (ko-sār'); cocinar (ko-see-nar')

cooked — cocido (ko-see'-do)

cookie — la galleta (la ga-yā'-ta)

cool — fresco (frās'-ko)

copper — el cobre (āl ko'-brā)

copy — la copia (la ko'-pya)

cork — el corcho (āl kor'-cho)

corkscrew — el sacacorchos (āl sa-ka-kor'-chos)

corn — el maíz (āl ma-ees')

corn on the cob — el elote (āl ā-lo'-tā)

corner — el rincón (āl reen-kon'); la esquina (la ās-kee'-na)

correct — correcto (ko-rrāk'-to)

corridor — el pasillo (āl pa-see'-yo)

74

cost — el precio (āl prā'-syo)

to cost — costar (kos-tar')

cotton — el algodón (āl al-go-don')

cough — la tos (la tos)

to cough — toser (to-sar')

to count — contar (kon-tar')

counter — el mostrador (āl mos-tra-dor')

country — el país (āl pa-ees'); el campo (āl kam'-po)

courage — el valor (āl ba-lor')

course — el curso (āl koor'-so)

court — el tribunal (āl tree-boo-nal')

cousin — el primo (āl pree'-mo)

to cover — cubrir (koo-breer')

cow — la vaca (la ba'-ka)

crab — el cangrejo (āl kan-grā'-ho)

cramp — el calambre (āl ka-lam'-brā)

crazy — loco (lo'-ko)

cream — la crema (la krā'-ma); la nata (la na'-ta)

credit card — la tarjeta de crédito (la tar-hā'-ta dā krā'-dee-to)

crew — la tripulación (la tree-poo-la-syon')

cross — la cruz (la croos)

to cross — atravesar (a-tra-bā-sar')

crossing — la travesía (la tra-bā-see'-ya)

crowd — el muchedumbre (āl moo-chā-doom'-brā); el gentío (āl hān-tee'-yo)

to cry — llorar (yo-rar')

cucumber — el pepino (āl pā-pee'-no); cohombro (co-om-bro)

cufflinks — los gemelos (los hā-mā'-los)

cup — la taza (la ta'-sa)

cure — la cura (la koo'-ra)

to cure — curar (koo-rar')

to curl — rizar (ree-sar')

current — la corriente (la ko-rryān'-tā)

curtain — la cortina (la kor-tee'-na)

curve — la curva (la koor'-ba)

custard — el flan (āl flan)

customer — el cliente (āl klee-ān'-tā)

customs — la aduana (la a-dwa'-na)

cut — la cortadura (la kor-ta-door'-a)

to cut — cortar (kor-tar')

cutlet — la chuleta (la choo-lā'-ta)

cylinder — el cilindro (āl see-leen'-dro)

daily — diario (dee-a'-ree-o)

to damage — hacer daño (a-sār' dan'-yo)

damaged — dañado (dan-ya'-do)

damp — húmedo (oo'-mā-do)

dance — el baile (āl bay'-lā)

to dance — bailar (bay-lar')

danger — el peligro (āl pā-lee'-gro)

dangerous — peligroso (pā-lee-gro'-so)

to dare — osar (o-sar'); atreverse (a-trā-bār'-sā)

dark — oscuro (o-skoo'-ro)

darkness — la oscuridad (la o-skoo-ree-dad')

date — la fecha (la fā'-cha)

date (fruit) — el dátil (āl da'-teel)

daughter — la hija (la ee'-ha)

day — el día (āl dee'-ya)

dead — muerto (mwār'-to)

deaf — sordo (sor'-do)

dear — querido (kā-ree'-do)

December — diciembre (dee-syām'-brā)

to decide — decidir (dā-see-deer')

deck — la cubierta (la koo-byār'-ta)

deck chair — la silla de cubierta (la see'-ya dā koo-byār'-ta)

to declare — declarar (dā-kla-rar')

deep — profundo (pro-foon'-do); hondo (on'-do)

deer — el venado (āl bā-na'-do)

delay — la demora (la dā-mo'-ra)

delicious — delicioso (dā-lee-syo'-so)

delighted — encantado (ān-kan-ta'-do)

to deliver — entregar (ān-trā-gar')

delivery — la entrega (la ān-trā'-ga)

dentist — el dentista (āl dān-tees'-ta)

dentures — la dentadura postiza (la dān-ta-doo'-ra)

deodorant — el desodorante (āl dās-o-do-ran'-tā)

department store — el almacén (āl al-ma-sān')

to descend — bajar (ba-har')

to describe — describir (dās-kree-beer')

desert — el desierto (āl dā-syār'-to)

desk — el escritorio (āl ās-kree-to'-ryo)

dessert — el postre (āl pos'-trā)

to destroy — destruir (dās-troo-weer')

detour — la desviación (la dās-bya-syon')

to develop (film) — revelar (rā-bā-lar')

to develop — desarrollar (dās-a-rroy-yar')

diabetic — diabético (dee-a-bā'-tee-ko)

to dial — marcar (mar-kar')

diamond — el diamante (āl dee-a-man'-tā)

diaper — el pañal (āl pan-yal')

diarrhea — la diarrea (la dee-ya-rrā'-a)

dictionary — el diccionario (āl deek-syo-na'-ryo)

to die — morir (mo-reer')

diet — la dieta (la dyā'-ta)

different — diferente (dee-fā-rān-tā)

difficult — difícil (dee-fee'-seel)

to dine — cenar (sā-nar')

dining car — el carro comedor (āl ka'-rro ko-mā-dor')

dining room — el comedor (āl ko-mā-dor')

dinner — la cena (la sā'-na)

direct — directo (dee-rāk'-to)

direction — la dirección (la dee-rāk-syon')

directory — la guía telefónica (la gee'-ya tā-lā-fo'-nee-ka)

dirty — sucio (soo'-syo)

to disappear — desaparacer (dās-a-pa-rā-sār')

discount — la rebaja (la rā-ba'-ha); el descuento (āl dās-kwān'-to)

to discuss — discutir (dees-koo-teer')

disease — la enfermedad (la ān-fār-mā-dad')

to disembark — desembarcar (dees-ām-bar-kar')

dish — el plato (āl pla'-to)

distance — la distancia (la dees-tan'-sya)

distributor — el distribuidor (āl dees-tree-bwee-dor')
district — el barrio (āl ba ͺ-rryo)
to disturb — molestar (mo-lās-tar')
dizzy — mareado (ma-rā-a ͺ-do)
to do — hacer (a-sār')
dock — el muelle (āl mwā ͺ-yā)
doctor — el doctor (āl dok-tor'); el médico (āl mā ͺ-dee-ko)
dog — el perro (āl pā ͺ-rro)
doll — la muñeca (la moon-yā ͺ-ka)
dollar — el dólar (āl do ͺ-lar)
done — hecho (ā ͺ-cho)
donkey — el burro (āal boo ͺ-rro)
door — la puerta (la pwār ͺ-ta)
dose — la dosis (la do ͺ-sees)
double — doble (do ͺ-blā)
double bed — cama matrimonial (la ka ͺ-ma ma-tree-mo-nyal')
doubt — la duda (la doo ͺ-da)
no doubt — sin duda (seen doo ͺ-da)
to doubt — dudar (doo-dar')
down — abajo (ā-ba ͺ-ho)
downstairs — abajo (a-ba ͺ-ho); el el piso bajo (ān āal pee ͺ-so ba ͺ-ho)
downtown — el centro (āl sān ͺ-tro)
dozen — la docena (la do-sā ͺ-na)
to draw out — sacar (sa-kar')
drawer — el cajón (āl ka-hon')
dress — el vestido (āl bās-tee ͺ-do)
to dress — vestirse (bās-teer ͺ-sā)
dressmaker — la modista (la mo-dees ͺ-ta)
dressing gown — la bata (la ba ͺ-ta)
drink — la bebida (la bā-bee ͺ-da)
to drink — beber (bā-bār')
drinkable — potable (po-ta ͺ-blā)
to drip — gotear (go-tā-yar')
to drive — manejar (ma-nā-har')
drier — el chófer (āl cho ͺ-fār); el conductor (āl kon-dook-tor')

driver's license — la licencia de manejar (la lee-sān'-sya dā ma-nā-har')

drug — la droga (la dro'-ga)

drug store — la farmacia (la far-ma'-sya)

drunk — borracho (bo-rra'-cho)

dry — seco (sā'-ko)

to dry — secar (sā-kar')

dry cleaner — la tintorería (la teen-to-rā-ree'-ya)

duck — el pato (āl pa'-to)

during — durante (doo-ran'-tā)

duty — el deber (āl dā-bār')

duty (tax) — el impuesto (āl eem-pwās'-to)

dysentery — la disentería (la dees-āan-tā-ree'-ya)

each — cada (ka'-da)

each one — cada uno (ka'-da oo'-no)

ear — el oído (āl o-ee'-do)

earache — el dolor de oído (āl do-lor' dā o-ee'-do)

early — temprano (tām-pra'-no)

to earn — ganar (ga-nar')

earring — el arete (āl a-rā'-tā)

earth — la tierra (la tyā'-rra)

easily — fácilmente (fa-seel-mān'-tā)

east — el este (āl ās'-tā)

easy — fácil (fa'-seel)

to eat — comer (ko-mār')

edge — el borde (āl bor'-dā)

eel la anguila (la an-gee'-la)

egg — el huevo (āl wā'-bo)

eight — ocho ('-cho)

eighteen — dieciocho (dyās-ee-o'-cho)

eighty — octavo (ok-ta'-bo)

eighty — ochenta (o-chān'-ta)

either — cualquiera (kwal-kyā'-ra)

elastic — elástico (ā-las'-tee-ko)

elbow — el codo (āl ko'-do)

electric — eléctrico (ā-lāk'-tree-ko)

èlevator — el ascensor (āl a-sān-sor')

eleven — once (on'-sā)

elsewhere — en otra parte (ān oᴸ-tra parᴸ-tā)

to embark — embarcar (ām-bar-kar')

embassy — la embajada (la ām-ba-ha'-da)

to embrace — abrazar (a-bra-sar')

emergency — la urgencia (la oor-hānᴸ-sya); la emergencia
(la āa-mār-hānᴸ-sya)

empty — vacío (ba-seeᴸ-yo)

end — el fin (āl feen)

to endores — endorsar (ān-do-sar')

engine — el motor (āl mo-tor'); la máquina (la maᴸ-kee-na)

England — Inglaterra (een-gla-tāᴸ-rra)

English — inglés (een-glās')

to enjoy — gozar (go-sar')

enlargement — la ampliación (la am-plee-a-syon')

enormous — bastante (bas-tanᴸ-tā)

to enter — entrar (ān-trar')

entertaining — divertido (dee-bār-teeᴸ-do)

entrance — la entrada (la ān-traᴸ-da)

envelope — el sobre (āl soᴸ-brā)

epileptic — epiléptico (ā-pee-lāpᴸ-tee-ko)

equal — igual (ee-gual')

equipment — el equipo (āl ā-keeᴸ-po)

error — el error (āl ā-rror')

Europe — Europa (ā-oo-roᴸ-pa)

even — aun (aoon); hasta (asᴸ-ta)

evening — la tarde (la tarᴸ-dā); la noche (la noᴸ-chā)

ever — alguna vez (al-gooᴸ-na bās)

every — cada (kaᴸ-da)

everybody — todo el mundo (toᴸ-do āl moonᴸ-do)

everything — todo (toᴸ-do)

everywhere — en todas partes (ān toᴸ-das parᴸ-tās); por
todas partes (por toᴸ-das parᴸ-tās)

evidently — evidentemente (ā-bee-dān-ta-mānᴸ-tā)

to examine — examinar (āk-sa-mee-nar')

example — el ejemplo (āl ā-hāmᴸ-plo)

excellent — excelente (āk-sā-lānᴸ-tā)

except — excepto (āk-sāpᴸ-to); menos (māᴸ-nos)

excess — el exceso (āl āk-sāᴸ-so)

exchange — el cambio (āl kam^L-byo)

excursion — la excursión (la āks-koor-syon')

to excuse — perdonar (pār-do-nar')

excercise — ejercicio (āl ā-hār-see^L-syo)

to exhaust — agotar (a-go-tar')

exhaust pipe — el tubo de escape /āl too^L-bo dā ās-ka^L-pā)

exhibit — la exposición (la āks-op-see-syon')

exit — la salida (la sa-lee^L-da)

to expect — esperar (ās-pā-rar')

expensive — caro (ka^L-ro)

to explain — explicar (āks-lee-kar')

explanation — la explicación (la āks-plee-ka-syon')

to export — exportar (āks-por-tar')

express — urgente (oor-hān^L-tā)

expressway — la autopista (la aoo-to-pees^L-ta)

extra — extra (āks^L-tra)

extraordinary — extraordinario (āks-tra-or-dee-na^L-ree-yo)

eye — el ojo (āl o^L-ho)

facade — la fachada (la fa-cha^L-da)

face — la cara (la ka^L-ra); el rostro (āl ros^L-tro)

factory — la fábrica (la fa^L-bree-ka)

to faint — desmayarse (dās-may-yar^L-sā)

fair — la feria (la fā^L-rya)

fair (blond) — rubio (roo^L-byo)

fall (season) — en otoño (āl o-ton^L-yo)

fall — la caída (la ka-ee^L-da)

to fall — caer (ka-ār')

false — falso (fal^L-so)

famila — la familia (la fa-mee^L-lya)

famous — famoso (fa-mo^L-so)

fan — el abanico (āl a-ba-nee^L-ko)

fan belt — la correa del ventilador (la ko-rrā^L-a dā
bān-tee-la-dor')

far — lejos (lā^L-hos)

fare — la tarifa (la ta-ree^L-fa)

farm — la granja (la gran^L-ha); la finca (la feen^L-ka)

farther — más lejos (mas lā^L-hos)

fashion — la moda (la mo^L-da)

fast — rápido (ra'-pee-do)

to fasten — fijar (fee-har')

fat — gordo (gor'-do)

father — el padre (āl pad'-rā)

father-in-law — el suegro (āl swā'-gro)

fault — la culpa (la kool'-pa)

favor — el favor (āl fa-bor')

favorite — el favorito (āl fa-bo-ree'-to)

fear — el miedo (āl myā'-do)

to fear — temer (tā-mār')

feather — la pluma (la ploo'-ma)

February — febrero (fā-brā'-ro)

fee — la tarifa (la ta-ree'-fa)

to feel — sentir(se) (sān-teer'-sā)

feeling — el sentimineto (āl sān-tee-myān'-to)

female — la hembra (la ām'-bra)

fence — la cerca (la sār'-ka)

fender — el guardafango (āl gwar-da-fan'-go)

ferry — el barco de trasbordo (āl bar'-ko dā tras-bor'-do)

fever — la fiebre (la fyā'-brā)l la calentura (la ka-lān-too'-ra)

few — pocos (po'-kos)

field — el campo (āl kam'-po)

fifteen — quince (keen'-sā)

fifth — quinto (keen'-to)

fifty — cincuenta (seen-kwān'-ta)

fig — el higo (āl ee'-go)

fight — la pelea (la pā-lā'-a)

to fight — pelear (pā-lā-ar')

fillet — el filete (āl fee-lā'-tā)

to fill — llenar (yā-nar')

filling (tooth) — el empaste (āl ām-pas'-tā)

film — la película (la pā-lee'-koo-la)

filter — el filtro (āl feel'-tro)

final — final (fee-nal')

finally — finalmente (fee-nal-mān'-tā)

to find — encontrar (ān-kon-trar')

fine — la multa (la mool'-ta)

82

fine — fino (fee'-no)

finger — el dedo (āl dā'-do)

to finish — terminar (tār-mee-nar'); acabar (a-ka-bar')

fire — el fuego (āl fwā'-go); el incendio (āl een-sān'-dyo)

to fire (from the job) — despedir (dās-pā-deer'); echar (ā-char')

first — primero (pree-mā-ro)

fish — el pescado (āl pās-ka'-do)

to fish — pescar (pās-kar')

marinated fish — el ceviche (āl sā-bee'-chā)

fisherman — el pescador (āl pās-ka-dor')

fishmarket — la pescadería (la pās-ka-dā-ree'-ya)

to fit — ajustar (a-hoos-tar')

five — cinco (seen'-ko)

five hundred — quinientos (keen-yān'-tos)

to fix — reparar (rā-pa-rar'); arreglar (a-rrā-glar')

flag — la bandera (la ban-dā'-ra)

flash bulb — la bombilla de flash (la bom-bee'-ya dā flash)

flash cubes — los cubitos de flash (los koo-bee'-tos dā flash)

flat — llano (ya'-no)

flat (tire) — desinflada (dās-een-fla'-da)

flight — el vuelo (āl bwā'-lo)

flint — la pedernal (la pā-dār-nal')

to flirt — coquetear (ko-kā-tā-yar')

flood — la inundación (la ee-noon-da-syon')

floor — el suelo (āl swā'-lo); el piso (āl pee'-so)

florist — el florero (āl flo-rā'-ro)

flower — la flor (la flor)

flu — la gripe (la gree'-pā)

fluid — fluído (floo'-ee-do)

fly — la mosca (la mos'-ka)

to fly — volar (bo-lar')

fog — la niebla (la nyā'-bla)

folk art — la artesanía (la ar-tā-sa-nee'-ya)

to follow — seguir (sā-geer')

following — siguiente (see-gyān'-tā)

food — la comida (la ko-mee'-da)

food poisoning — la intoxicación (la een-tok-see-ka-syon')
(on) foot — (a) pie (a pee'-ā)
football — el futból (āl foot-bol')
for — para (pa'-ra); por (por)
to forbid — prohibir (pro-ee-beer')
forbidden — prohibido (pro-ee-bee'-do)
forehead — la frente (la frān'-tā)
foreign — extranjero (ās-tran-hā'-ro)
forest — el bosque (āl bos'-kā)
to forget — olvidar (ol-bee-dar')
to forgive — perdonar (pār-do-nar')
fork — el tenedor (āl tā-nā-dor')
form — la forma (la for'-ma)
former — anterior (an-tā-ryor')
fort — el fuerte (āl fwār'-tā); la fortaleza (la for-ta-lā'-sa)
fortress — la fortaleza (la for-ta-lā'-sa)
fortunate — afortunado (a-for-too-na'-do)
fortunately — afortunadamente (a-for-too-na-da-mān'-tā)
forty — cuarenta (kwa-rān'-ta)
fountain — la fuente (la fwān'-tā)
forward — adelante (a-dā-lan'-tā)
four — cuatro (kwa'-tro)
fourteen — catorce (ka-tor'-sā)
fourth — cuarto (kwar'-to)
fracture — la fractura (la frak-too'-ra)
fragile — frágil (fra'-heel)
France — Francia (fran'-sya)
free — libre (lee'-brā); gratis (gra'-tees)
freedom — la libertad (la lee-bār-tad')
to freeze — helarse (ā-lar'-sā)
French — francés (fran-sās')
frequently — frecuentemente (frā-kwān-ta-mān'-tā)
fresh — fresco (frās'-ko)
Friday — el viernes (āl byār'-nās)
fried — frito (free'-to)
friend — el amigo (āl a-mee'-go)
friendly — amistoso (a-mees-to'-so)
from — de (dā)

front — frente (frān⌐-tā)

(in) front (of) — delante de (dā-lan⌐-tā dā)

frontier — la frontera (la fron-tā⌐-ra)

frozen — helado (ā-la⌐-do)

fruit — la fruta (la froo⌐-ta)

fuel pump — la bomba de combustible (la bom⌐-ba dā
kom-boos-tee⌐-blā)

full — lleno (yā⌐-no); completo (kom-plā⌐-to)

fun — la diversión (la dee-bār-syon')

function — la función (la foon-syon')

funnel — el embudo (āl ām-boo⌐-do)

funny — cómico (ko⌐-mee-ko)

fur — la piel (la pyāl)

furnished — amueblado (a-mwā-bla⌐-do)

furniture — los muebles (los mwā⌐-blās)

further — más lejos (mas lā⌐-hos); más adelante (más
a-dā-lan⌐-tā)

future — el futuro (āl foo-too⌐-ro)

to gain — ganar (ga-nar')

gallery — la galería (la ga-lā-ree⌐-ya)

to gamble — jugar (hoo-gar')

game — el juego (āl hwā⌐-go)

garage — el garage (āl ga-ra⌐-hā)

garden — el jardín (āl har-deen')

garlic — el ajo (āl a⌐-ho)

gasoline — la gasolina (la ga-so-lee⌐-na)

gas station — la gasolinera (la ga-so-lee-nā⌐-ra); el puesto
de gasolina (āl pwās⌐-to dā ga-so-lee⌐-na)

gate — la puerta (la pwār⌐-ta)

to gather — recoger (rā-ko-hār')

gay (happy) — alegre (a-lā⌐-grā)

general — general (hā-nā-ral')

general delivery — la lista de correos (la lees⌐-ta dā
ko-rrā⌐-os)

generous — generoso (hā-nā-ros⌐-o)

gentleman — el caballero (āl ka-ba-yā⌐-ro)

German — alemán (a-lā-man')

Germany — Alemania (a-lā-ma⌐-nya)

to get — obtener (ob-tā-nār'); coger (ko-hār')

to get off — bajar (ba-har')

to get on — subir (soo-beer')

to get up — levantarse (lā-ban-tar'-sā)

gift — el regalo (āl rā-gaᴸ-lo)

gin — la ginebra (la hee-nāᴸ-bra)

girl — la muchacha (la moo-chaᴸ-cha)

to give — dar (dar)

glad — contento (kon-tānᴸ-to)

gladly — con mucho gusto (kon mooᴸ-cho goosᴸ-to)

glass — el vaso (āl baᴸ-so)

glass (material) — el vidrio (āl beeᴸ-dryo)

glasses — las gafas (las gaᴸ-fas); los lentes (los lānᴸ-tās)

gloves — los guantes (los gwanᴸ-tās)

to go — ir (eer)

to go back — volver (bol-bār')

god — el dios (āl dee'yos)

goddess — la diosa (la dyoᴸ-sa)

gold — el oro (āl oᴸ-ro)

good — bueno (bwāᴸ-no)

good afternoon — buenas tardes (bwāᴸ-nas tarᴸ-dās)

good morning — buenos días (bwāᴸ-nos deeᴸ-yas)

good night — buenas noches (bwāᴸ-nas noᴸ-chās)

goodbye — adiós (a-dyos')

government — el gobierno (āl go-byārᴸ-no)

granddaughter — la nieta (la nyāᴸ-ta)

grandfather — el abuelo (āl a-bwāᴸ-lo)

grandmother — la abuela (la a-bwāᴸ-la)

grandson — el nieto (āl nyāᴸ-to)

grape — la uva (la ooᴸ-ba)

grapefruit — la toronja (la to-ronᴸ-ha); pomelo (po-māᴸ-lo)

grass — la hierba (la yārᴸ-ba)

grateful — agradecido (a-gra-dā-seeᴸ-do)

gray — gris (grees)

grease — la grasa (la graᴸ-sa)

to grease — engrasar (ān-gra-sar')

great — grande (granᴸ-dā)

green — verde (bārᴸ-dā)

grilled — a la plancha (a la plan'-cha); a la parrilla (a la
pa-rree'-ya)

groceries — los abarrotes (los a-ba-rro'-tās); los
comestibles (los ko-mās-tee'-blās)

ground — la tierra (la tyā'-rra)

ground (up) — molido (mo-lee'-do)

ground floor — el primer piso (āl pree-mār' pee'-so)

group — el grupo (āl groo'-po)

to grow — crecer (krā-sār')

to grow (like to grow vegetables) — cultivar
(cool-tee-var')

guarantee — la garantía (la ga-ran-tee'-ya)

to guard — guardar (gwar-dar')

guest — el huésped (āl wās'-pād)

guide — el guía (āl gee'-ya)

guidebook — la guía (la gee'-ya)

guilty — culpable (kool-pa'-blā)

guitar — la guitarra (la gee-ta'-rra)

gum — el chicle (āl chee'-klā); la goma (la go'-ma)

gun — el fusil (āl foo-seel'); la pistola (la pees-to'-la)

habit — la costumbre (la kos-toom'-brā)

hair — el pelo (āl pā'-lo)

hairbrush — el cepillo para el pelo (āl sā-pee'-yo pa'-ra āl
pā'-lo)

haircut — el corte de pelo (āl kor'-tā dā pā'-lo)

hairdresser's — la peluquería (la pā-loo-kā-ree'-ya)

hairpin — la horquilla (la or-kee'-ya)

half — medio (mā'-dyo); la mitad (la mee-tad')

hall — el corredor (āl ko-rrā-dor')

ham — el jamón (āl ha-mon')

hand — la mano (la ma'-no)

handkerchief — el pañuelo (āl pan-ywāl'-lo)

handmade — hecho a mano (ā'-cho a ma'-no)

handsome — guapo (gwa'-po)

to hang — colgar (kol-gar')

hanger — la percha (la pār'-cha)

to happen — suceder (soo-sā-dār')

happy — feliz (fā-lees')

harbor — el puerto (āl pwār^L-to)

hard — duro (doo^L-ro)

harm — el daño (āl dan^L-yo)

to harm — dañar (dan-yar')

harmful — dañino (dan-yee^L-no); dañoso (dan-yo^L-so)

haste — la prisa (la pree^L-sa)

hat — el sombrero (āl som-brā^L-ro)

hat store — la sombrerería (la som-brā-rā-ree^L-ya)

to hate — odiar (o-dee-yar')

to have — tener (tā-nār')

to have (auxiliary verb) — haber (a-bār')

to have to — deber (dā-bār'); tener que (tā-nār' kā)

hay — el heno (āl ā^L-no); la paja (la pa^L-ha)

hay fever — el catarro asmático (āl ka-ta^L-rro
as-ma^L-tee-ko)

he — él (āl)

head — la cabeza (la ka-bā^L-sa)

headache — el dolor de cabeza (āl do-lor' dā ka-bā^L-sa)

health — la salud (la sa-lood')

to hear — oír (o-eer')

heart — el corazón (āl ko-ra-son')

heat — el calor (āl ka-lor')

heating — la calefacción (la ka-lā-fak-syon')

heavy — pesado (pā-sa^L-do)

heel — el tacón (āl ta-kon')

heel (foot) — el talón (āl ta-lon')

hello — hola (o^L-la)

hello? (telephone) — ¿bueno? (bwā^L-no); ¿diga? (dee^L-ga)

help — la ayuda (la a-yoo^L-da)

help! — ¡socorro! (so-ko^L-rro); ¡auxilio! (aook-see^L-lyo)

to help — ayudar (a-yoo-dar')

helpful — útil (oo^L-teel)

hem — el dobladillo (āl do-bla-dee^L-yo); la bastilla (la
bas-tee^L-ya)

hen — la gallina (la ga-yee^L-na)

her — la (la); su (soo)

here — aquí (a-kee')

herring — el arenque (āl a-rān^L-kā)

hers — suyo (soo⌐yo)
high — alto (al⌐to)
higher up — más arriba (mas a-rree⌐ba)
highway — la carretera (la ka-rrā-tā⌐ra)
hill — la colina (la ko-lee⌐na); la loma (la lo⌐ma)
him — él (āl)
hip — la cadera (la ka-dā⌐ra)
to hire — alquilar (āl-kee-lar'); arrendar (a-rrān-dar')
his — su (soo); suyo (soo⌐yo)
history — la historia (la ees-to⌐ree-ya)
to hit — pegar (pā-gar')
to hold — tener (tā-nār')
hole — el agujero (āl a-goo-hā⌐ro); el hoyo (āl oy⌐yo)
holy — santo (san⌐to)
(at) home — (en) casa (ān ka⌐sa)
home — el hogar (āl o-gar')
honest — honrado (on-ra⌐do)
honey — la miel (la myāal)
honor — el honor (āl o-nor')
hope — la esperanza (la ās-pā-ran⌐sa)
to hope — esperar (ās-pā-ra)
horn (car) — la bocina (la bo-see⌐na); la trompa (la trom⌐pa)
hors d'oeuvres — los entremeses (los ān-trā-mā⌐sās)
horse — el caballo (āl ka-ba⌐yo)
hospital — el hospital (āl os-pee-tal')
host — el anfitrión (āl an-fee-tree-yon')
hot — caliente (kal-yān⌐tā)
hot (spicy) — picante (pee-kan⌐tā)
hotel — el hotel (āl o-tāl')
hour — la hora (la o⌐ra)
house — la casa (la ka⌐sa)
how — cómo (ko⌐mo)
how many — cuántos (kwan⌐tos)
how much — cuánto (kwan⌐to)
hug — el abrazo (āl a-bra⌐so)
human — humano (oo-ma⌐no)
humid — húmedo (oo⌐mā-do)

hundred — cien(to) (syān'-to)

hunger — el hambre (āl am'-brā)

to be hungry — tener hambre (tā-nār' am'-brā)

to be in a hurry — tener prisa (tā-nār' pree'-sa)

hurry! — ¡de prisa! (dā pree'-sa)

to hurt — doler (do-lār'); lastimar (las-tee-mar')

husband — el esposo (āl ās-po'-so); el marido (āl ma-ree'-do)

I — yo (yo)

ice — el hielo (āl yā'-lo)

ice cream — el helado (āl ā-la'-do)

idea — la idea (la ee-dā'-a)

identification — la identificación (la ee-dān-tee-fee-ka-syon')

if — si (see)

ignition — el encendido (āl ān-sān-dee'-do); la ignición (la eeg-nee-syon')

ill — enfermo (ān-fār'-mo)

illegal — ilegal (ee-lā-gal')

illness — la enfermedad (la ān-fār-mā-dad')

to imagine — imaginar (ee-ma-hee-nar')

immediately — inmediatamente (een-mā-dya-ta-mān'-tā)

important — importante (eem-por-tan'-tā)

impossible — imposible (eem-po-see'-blā)

to improve — mejorar (mā-ho-rar')

in — en (ān)

incident — el incidente (āl een-see-dān'-tā)

to include — incluir (een-kloo-weer')

included — incluído (een-kloo-ee'-do)

incomplete — incompleto (een-kom-plā'-to)

inconvenient — incómodo (een-ko'-mo-do)

incorrect — erróneo (ā-rron'-ā-o); incorrecto (een-ko-rrāk'-to)

to increase — aumentar (aoo-mān-tar')

incredible — increíble (een-krā-ee'-blā)

indeed — de veras (dā bā'-ras); realmente (rā-al-mān'-tā)

independence — la independencia (la een-dā-pān-dān'-see-ya)

to indicate — indicar (een-dee-kar')

indigestion — la indigestión (la een-dee-hās-tyon')

indoors — en casa (ān ka¹-sa); adentro (a-dān¹-tro)

industrial — industrial (een-doos-tree-yal')

inexpensive — barato (ba-ra¹-to)

infection — la infección (la een-fāk-syon')

influenza — la gripe (la gree¹-pā)

information — la información (la een-for-ma-syon')

to inform — informar (een-for-mar')

injection — la inyección (la een-yāk-syon')

injury — el daño (āl dan¹-yo); la herida (la ā-ree¹-da)

ink — la tinta (la teen¹-ta)

inn — la posada (la po-sa¹-da)

to inquire — preguntar (prā-goon-tar')

insect — el insecto (āl een-sāk¹-to)

insect bite — la picadura de insecto (la pee-ka-doo¹-ra dā
   een-sāk¹-to)

inside — dentro de (dān¹-tro dā)

to insist — insistir (een-sees-teer')

to inspect — revisar (rā-bee-sar')

instead of — en lugar de (ān loo-gar' dā)

institution — la institución (la een-stee-too-syon')

insurance — el seguro (āl sā-goo¹-ro)

to insure — asegurar (a-sā-goo-rar')

intelligent — inteligente (een-tā-lee-hān¹-tā)

to intend — intentar (een-tān-tar')

intense — intenso (een-tān¹-so)

intention — la intención (la een-tān-syon')

interest — el interés (āl een-tā-rās')

to interest — interesar (een-tā-rā-sar')

interesting — interesante (een-tā-rā-san¹-tā)

intermission — entreacto (ān¹-trā-ak¹-to); la intermedio (āl
   een-tār-mee-deeo')

internal — interno (een-tār¹-no)

international — internacional (een-tār-na-syo-nal')

to interpret — interpretar (een-tār-prā-tar')

interpreter — el intérprete (āl een-tār¹-prā-tā)

interview — la entrevista (la ān-trā-bees¹-ta)

into — en (ān)

to introduce — presentar (prā-sān-tar')

introduction — la introducción (la een-tro-dook-syon')

to investigate — investigar (een-bās-tee-gar')

invitation — la invitación (la een-bee-ta-syon')

to invite — invitar (een-bee-tar')

Ireland — Irlanda (eer-lan'-da)

Irish — irlandés (eer-lan-dās')

iron — la plancha (la plan'-cha)

iron (metal) — el hierro (āl yā'-rro)

to iron — planchar (plan-char')

island — la isla (la ees'-la)

it — él (āl); ella (ā'-ya); lo (lo); la (la)

it is — es (ās); está (ās-ta')

Italian — italiano (ee-tal-ya'-no)

Italy — Italia (ee-tal'-ya)

jacket — la chaqueta (la cha-kā'-ta)

jade — el jade (āl ha'-dā)

jail — la cárcel (la kar'-sāl)

jam — la mermelada (la mār-mā-la'-da)

January — enero (ā-nā'-ro)

jar — el frasco (āl fras'-ko); la jarra (la ha'-rra)

jaw — la mandíbula (la man-dee'-boo-la)

jelly — la mermelada (la mār-mā-la'-da); la jalea (la ha-lā'-a)

jellyfish — la medusa (la mā-doo'-sa)

jewel — la joya (la hoy'-ya)

jewelry store — la joyería (la hoy-ā-ree'-ya)

job — el empleo (āl ām-plā'-o)

joke — la broma (la bro'-ma)

journey — el viaje (āl bya'-hā)

jug — el jarro (āl ha'-rro)

juice — el jugo (āl hoo'-go)

July — julio (hoo'-lyo)

to jump — saltar (sal-tar')

June — junio (hoo'-nyo)

just — justo (hoos'-to)

(to have) just — acabar de (a-ka-bar' dā)

justice — la justicia (la hoos-tee'-sya)

to keep — conservar (kon-sär-bar'); guardar (gwar-dar')

key — la llave (la ya'-bā)

kid (animal)

el cabrito (āl ka-bree'-to)

kidney — el riñon (āl reen-yon')

to kill — matar (ma-tar')

kilogram — el kilogramo (āl kee-lo-gra'-mo)

kilometer — el kilómetro (āl kee-lo'-mā-tro)

kind — amable (a-ma'-blā)

kind — la especie (la ās-pā'-sya)

king — el rey (āl rā-ee)

kiss — el beso (āl bā'-so)

to kiss — besar (bā-sar')

kitchen — la cocina (la ko-see'-na)

knee — la rodilla (la ro-dee'-ya)

knife — el cuchillo (āl koo-chee'-yo)

to know (someone) — conocer (ko-no-sār')

to know (something) — saber (sa-bār')

label — la etiqueta (la ā-tee-kā'-ta); el marbete (āl mar-bā'-tā)

laborer — el trabajador (āl tra-ba-ha-dor')

lace — el encaje (āl ān-ka'-hā)

ladder — la escalera (la ās-ka-lā'-ra)

lady — la dama (la da'-ma); la señora (la sān-yo'-ra)

lake — el lago (āl la'-go)

lamb — el cordero (āl kor-dā'-ro)

lame — cojo (ko'-ho)

lamp — la lámpara (la lam'-pa-ra)

land — la tierra (la tyā'-rra)

to land — aterrizar (ā-tā-rree-sar')

landlord — el propietario (āl pro-pee-ā-ta'-ryo); el dueño (āl dwān'-yo)

language — el idioma (āl ee-dyo'-ma)

large — grande (gran'-dā)

last — último (ool'-tee-mo)

to last — durar (doo-rar)

last year — el año pasado (āl an'-yo pa-sa'-do)

late — tarde (tar'-dā)
later — más tarde (mas tar'-dā); luego (lwā'-go)
laugh — la risa (la ree'-sa)
to laugh — reír (rā-eer')
laundry — la lavandería (la la-ban-dā-ree'-ya)
lavatory — el retrete (āl rā-trā'-tā); el lavatorio (āl la-ba-to'-ryo)
law — la ley (la lā-ee)
lawyer — el abogado (āl a-bo-ga'-do)
laxative — el laxante (āl lak-san'-tā)
lazy — perezoso (pā-rā-so'-so)
lead — el plomo (āl plo'-mo)
to lead — conducir (kon-doo-seer')
leaf — la hoja (la o'-ha)
to leak — gotear (go-tā-yar')
to learn — aprender (a-prān-dār')
least — mínimo (mee'-nee-mo)
leather — la piel (la pyāl); el cuero (āl-coo-ā'-ro)
to leave — dejar (dā-har'); salir (sa-leer')
Leave me alone! — ¡Déjeme! (dā'-hā-mā)
left — izquierda (ees-kyār'-da)
leg — la pierna (la pyār'-na)
lemon — el limón (āl lee-mon')
lemonade — la limonada (la lee-mo-na'-da)
to lend — prestar (prās-tar')
length — el largo (āl lar'-go)
lens — el lente (āl lān'-tā); el objetivo (āl ob-hā-tee'-bo)
lens cap — la tapa del lente (la-ta'-pa)
lentils — las lentejas (las lān-tā'-has)
less — menos (mā'-nos)
to let — permitir (pār-mee-teer')
letter — la carta (la kar'-ta)
lettuce — la lechuga (la lā-choo'-ga)
liberty — la libertad (la lee-bar-tad')
library — la biblioteca (la bee-blee-o-tā'-ka)
license — la licencia (la lee-sān'-sya)
lie — la mentira (la mān-tee'-ra)
to lie down — acostarse (a-kos-tar'-sā)

life — la vida (la bee-ᴸda)

life preserver — el salvavidas (āl sal-ba-bee-ᴸdas)

to lift — levantar (lā-bān-tar')

light — la luz (la loos)

light (weight) — ligero (lee-hāᴸ-ro)

light meter — el exposímetro (āl āk-spo-see-ᴸmā-tro)

lighter — el encendedor (āl ān-sān-dā-dor')

lighthouse — el faro (āl faᴸ-ro)

lightning — el relámpago (āl rā-lamᴸ-pa-go)

(do you) like — le gusta (la goosᴸ-ta)

(I would) like — quisiera (kee-syāᴸ-ra)

lima bean — la haba (la aᴸ-ba)

lime — la lima (la leeᴸ-ma)

line — la línea (la leeᴸ-nā-ya)

linen — el lino (āl leeᴸ-no)

lip — el labio (āl laᴸ-byo)

lipstick — el lápiz de labios (āl laᴸ-pees dā los laᴸ-byos)

liquor — el licor (āl lee-kor')

liquor store — la tienda de licores (la tyānᴸ-da dā lee-koᴸ-rās)

list — la lista (la leesᴸ-ta)

to listen — escuchar (ās-koo-char')

liter — el litro (āl leeᴸ-tro)

little — poco (poᴸ-ko); pequeño (pā-kānᴸ-yo)

live — vivo (beeᴸ-bo)

to live — vivir (bee-beer')

liver — el hígado (āl eeᴸ-ga-do)

livestock — el ganado (āl ga-naᴸ-do)

lobby — el salón de entrada (āl sa-lon' dā ān-traᴸ-da)

lobster — la langosta (la lan-gosᴸ-ta)

local — local (lo-kal')

lock — la cerradura (la sā-rra-dooᴸ-ra)

to lodge — hospedarse (os-pā-dar'-sā)

long — largo (larᴸ-go)

long distance — larga distancia (larᴸ-ga dees-tanᴸ-sya)

to look (at) — mirar (mee-rar')

to look for — buscar (boos-kar')

Look out! — ¡Cuidado! (kwee-daᴸ-do)

loose — flojo (flo'-ho)
to lose — perder (pãr-dãr')
lost — perdido (par-dee'-do)
(a) lot — mucho (moo'-cho)
lotion — la loción (la lo-syon')
loud — ruidoso (roo-ee-do'-so)
love — el amor (ãl a-mor')
to love — amar (a-mar')
lovely — hermoso (ãr-mo'-so)
low — bajo (ba'-ho)
to lubricate — lubricar (loo-bree-kar')
luck — la suerte (la swãr'-tã)
(good) luck — buena suerte (bwã'-na swãr'-tã)
lucky — afortunado (a-for-too-na'-do)
luggage — el equipaje (ãl ã-kee-pa'-hã)
luggage ticket — el talón (ãl ta-lon')
lunch — el almuerzo (ãl al-mwãr'-so)
lung — el pulmón (ãl pool-mon')
machine — la máquina (la ma'-kee-na)
madam — señora (sãn-yo'-ra)
magazine — la revista (la rã' -bees'-ta)
maid — la camarera (la ka-ma-rã'-ra)
mail — el correo (ãl ko-rrã'-o)
mailbox — el buzón (ãl boo-son')
mailman — el cartero (ãl kar-tã'-ro)
main — principal (preen-see-pal')
major — mayor (may-yor')
to make — hacer (a-sãr')
make-up — el maquillaje (ãl ma-kee-ya'-hã); los
  cosméticos (los kos-mã'-tee-kos)
man — el hombre (ãl om'-brã); el señor (ãl sãn-yor')
manager — el gerente (ãl hã-rãn'-tã)
manicure — la manicure (la ma-nee-koo'-ra)
manufactured — manufacturado (ma-noo-fak-too-ra'-do);
  fabricado (fa-bree-ka'-do)
many — muchos (moo'-chos)
map — el mapa (ãl ma'-pa)
marble — el mármol (ãl mar'-mol)

marbles — las canicas (las ka-nee'-kas)

March — marzo (mar'-so)

margarine — la margarina (la mar-ga-ree'-na)

marinated — en escabeche (ān ās-ka-bā'-chā)

mark — la marca (la mar'-ka)

market — el mercado (āl mār-ka'-do)

marmalade — la mermelada (la mār-mā-la'-da)

married — casado (ka-sa'-do)

to marry — casarse (ka-sar'-sā)

marvelous — maravilloso (ma-ra-bee-yo'-so)

Mass — la misa (la mee'-sa)

massage — el masaje (āl ma-sa'-hā)

matches — los cerillos (los sā-ree'-yos); los fósforos (los fos'-fo-ros)

material — la tela (la tā'-la); el material (āl ma-tā-ryal')

to matter — importar (eem-por-tar')

mattress — el colchón (āl kol-chon')

maximum — máximo (mak'-see-mo)

May — mayo (ma'-yo)

mayonnaise — la mayonesa (la ma-yo-nā'-sa)

me — me (mā); mí (mee)

(with) me — conmigo (kon-mee'-go)

meal — la comida (la ko-mee'-da)

to mean — querer decir (kā-rā' dā-seer'); significar (seeg-nee-fee-kar')

measure — la medida (la mā-dee'-da)

to measure — medir (mā-deer')

meat — la carne (la kar'-nā)

meatballs — las albóndigas (las alb-bon-dee'-gas)

mechanic — el mecánico (āl mā-ka'-nee-ko)

medicine — la medicina (la mā-dee-see'-na)

to meet — conocer (ko-no-sār'); encontrar (ān-kon-trar')

melon — el melón (āl mā-lon')

member — el miembro (āl myām'-bro)

memory — la memoria (la mā-mo'-ree-a)

to mend — reparar (rā-pa-rar')

to mention — mencionar (mān-syo-nar')

menu — el menú (āl mā-noo')

message — el recado (āl rä-ka'-do); el mensaje (āl mān-sa'-hā)

messenger — el mensajero (āl mān-sa-hā'-ro)

metal — el metal (āl mä-tal')

meter — el metro (āl mä'-tro)

midday — el mediodía (āl mä-dyo-dee'-ya)

middle — el medio (āl mä'-dyo)

midnight — la medianoche (la mä-dya-no'-chā)

mild — blando (blan'-do)

milk — la leche (la lā'-chā)

million — millón (mee-yon')

mind — la mente (la mān'-tā)

I mind — me importa (mä-eem-por'-ta)

mine — mío (mee'-yo)

mineral water — el agua mineral (la a'-gwa mee-nä-ral')

minute — el minuto (āl mee-noo'-to)

mirror — el espejo (āl ās-pā'-ho)

misfortune — la desgracia (la dās-gra'-sya)

Miss — señorita (sān-yo-ree'-ta)

to miss — perder (pär-dār')

mistake — el error (āl ā-rror')

mistaken — equivocado (ā-kee-bo-ka'-do)

to mix — mezclar (mās-klar')

mixed — mezclado (mās-kla'-do)

model — el modelo (āl mo-dā'-lo)

modern — moderno (mo-dār'-no)

modest — modesto (mo-dās'-to)

molar — la muela (la mwä'-la)

moment — el momento (āl mo-mān'-to)

Monday — el lunes (āl loo'-nās)

money — el dinero (āl dee-nä'-ro)

money order — el giro postal (āl hee'-ro pos-tal')

monk — el monje (āl mon'-hā)

month — el mes (āl mās)

monument — el monumento (āl mo-noo-mān'-to)

moon — la luna (la loo'-na)

more — más (mas)

morning — la mañana (la man-ya'-na)

mosquito — el mosquito (āl mos-kee'-to)

most — el más (āl mas); la más (la mas)

mother — la madre (la ma'-drā)

motion — la moción (la mo-syon'); el movimiento (āl mo-bee-myān'-to)

motor — el motor (āl mo-tor')

motorcycle — la motocicleta (la mo-to-see-klā'-ta)

mountain — la montaña (la mon-tan'-ya)

mouth — la boca (la bo'-ka)

to move — mover (mo-bār')

movie — el cine (āl see'-nā)

movie film — la película del cine (la pā-lee'-koo-la dāl see'-nā)

Mr. — señor (sān-yor')

Mrs. — señora (sān-yo'-ra)

much — mucho (moo'-cho)

mud — el fango (āl fan'-go); el lodo (al lo'-do)

muffler — el silenciador (āl see-lān-see-ya-dor'); el mofle (āl mof'-lā)

muscle — el músculo (āl moos'-koo-lo)

museum — el museo (āl moo-sā'-yo)

mushrooms — los hongos (los on'-gos); los champiñones (los cham-peen-yo'-nās)

music — la música (la moo'-see-ka)

musician — el músico (āl moo'-see-ko)

must — deber (dā-bār'); tener que (tā-nār' kā)

mustache — el bigote (āl bee-go'-tā)

mustard — la mostaza (la mos-ta'-sa)

mutton — el carnero (āl kar-nā'-ro)

my — mi (mee)

myself — yo mismo (yo mees'-mo)

nail — el clavo (āl kla'-bo)

(finger) nail — la uña (la oon'-ya)

nail file — la lima de uñas (la lee'-ma dā oon'-yas)

name — el nombre (āl nom'-brā)

napkin — la servilleta (la sār-bee-yā'-ta)

narrow — angosto (an-gos'-to); estrecho (ās-trā'-cho)

nation — la nación (la na-syon')

national — nacional (na-syo-nal')
nationality — la nacionalidad (la na-syo-na-lee-dad')
native — nativo (na-tee'-bo)
natural — natural (na-too-ral')
naturally — naturalmente (na-too-ral-mān'-tā)
nature — la naturaleza (la na-too-ra-lā'-sā)
nausea — el asco (āl as'-ko); la naúsea (la naoo'-sā-a)
near — cerca (sār'-ka)
nearly — casi (ka'-see)
neck — el cuello (āl kwā'-yo)
necklace — el collar (āl ko-yar')
necktie — la corbata (la kor-ba'-ta)
to need — necesitar (nā-sā-see-tar')
needle — la aguja (la a-goo'-ha)
negative — la negativa (la nā-ga-tee'-ba)
neighbor — el vecino (āl bā-see'-no)
neighborhood — el barrio (āl ba'-rryo)
neither...nor — ni...ni (nee...nee)
nephew — el sobrino (āl so-bree'-no)
nerve — el nervio (āl nār'-byo)
nervous — nervioso (nār-byo'-so)
never — nunca (noon'-ka)
nevertheless — sin embargo (seen ām-bar'-go)
new — nuevo (nwā'-bo)
news — las noticias (las no-tee'-syas)
newspaper — el periódico (āl pa-ree-o'-dee-ko)
next — próximo (prok'-see-mo)
nice — simpático (seem-pa'-tee-ko)
night — la noche (la no'-chā)
nightgown — el camisón (āl ka-mee-son')
nine — nueve (nwāā'-bā)
nine hundred — novecientos (no-bā-syān'-tos)
nineteen — diecinueve (dyās-ee-nwā'-bā)
ninety — noventa (no-bān'-ta)
ninth — nono (no'-no); noveno (no-bā'-no)
no — no (no)
no one — nadie (na'-dyā)
nobody — nadie (na'-dyā)

noise — el ruido (āl rwee'-do)

noisy — ruidoso (rwee-do'-so)

none — ninguno (neen-goo'-no)

noon — mediodía (mā-dyo-dee'-ya)

north — norte (nor'-tā)

northeast — nordeste (nor-dās'-tā)

northwest — noroeste (nor-o-ās'-tā)

nose — la nariz (la na'-rees)

not — no (no)

note — la nota (la no'-ta)

notebook — el cuaderno (āl kwa-dār'-no)

nothing — nada (na'-da)

nothing else — nada más (na'-da mas)

notice — el aviso (āl a-bee'-so)

to notice — notar (no-tar')

nougat — el turrón (āl too-rron')

novel — la novela (la no-bā'-la)

November — noviembre (no-byām'-brā)

novocaine — la novocaína (la no-bo-ca-ee'-na)

now — ahora (a-o'-ra)

nowhere — en ninguna parte (ān neen-goo'-na par'-tā)

number — número (noo'-mā-ro)

nun — la monja (la mon'-ha)

nurse — la enfermera (la ān-fār-mā'-ra)

nursemaid — la niñera (la neen-yā'-ra); la nana (la na'-na)

nut — la nuez (la nwās)

nylon — el nilón (āl nee-lon')

omelet — la tortilla a la española (la tor-tee'-ya a la ās-pan-yo'-la)

on — en (ān) — **once** — una vez (oo'-na bās)

one — uno (oo'-no)

one way — de ida (dā ee'-da)

onion — la cebolla (la sā-boy'-ya)

only — solo (so'-lo); adv. sólo (so'-lo)

(the) only (one) — el único (āl oo'-nee-ko)

open — abierto (a-byār'-to)

to open — abrir (a-breer')

opera — la ópera (la o-pā-ra)

operation — la operación (la o-pā-ra-syon')

operator — la telefonista (la tā-lā-fo-nees'-ta); la operadora (la o-pā-ra-do'-ra)

opinion — la opinión (la o-peen-yon')

opportunity — la oportunidad (la o-por-too-nee-dad')

opposite — opuesto (o-pwās'-to)

optician — el óptico (āl op'-tee-ko)

or — o (o)

orange — la naranja (la na-ran'-ha)

orchestra — la orquesta (la or-kās'-ta)

order — el orden (āl orden (āl or-dān)

to order — pedir (pā-deer); ordenar (or-dā-nar')

ordinary — ordinario (or-dee-na'-ree-o)

oriental — oriental (o-ryān-tal')

original — original (o-ree-hee-nal')

ornament — el ornamento (āl or-na-mān'-to)

other — otro (o'-tro)

ought — deber (dā-bār')

our — nuestro (nwās'-tro)

out — fuera (fwā'-ra)

out of order — descompuesto (dās-kom-pwās'-to)

outside — afuera (a-fwā'-ra)

over — sobre (so'-brā)

over (ended) — terminado (tār-mee-na'-do)

over there — por allá (por a-ya')

overcoat — el abrigo (āl a-bree'-go)

overhead — arriba (a-ree'-ba)

to overturn — volcar (bol-kar')

to owe — deber (dā-bār')

own — propio (pro-pee'-o)

owner — el dueño (āl dwān'-yo)

oyster — la ostra (la os'-tra)

to pack — empaquetar (ām-pa-kā-tar'); empacar (ām-pa-kar')

package — el paquete (āl pa-kā'-tā)

page — la página (la pa'-hee-na)

paid — pagado (pa-ga'-do)

pain — el dolor (āl do-lor')

paint — la pintura (la peen-too¹-ra)

to paint — pintar (peen-tar')

painting — el cuadro (āl kwa¹-dro)

pair — el par (āl par); la pareja (la pa-rā¹-ha)

palace — el palacio (āl pa-la¹-syo)

pale — pálido (pa¹-lee-do)

palm — la palma (la pal¹-ma)

pants — los pantalones (los pan-ta-lo¹-nās)

paper — el papel (āl pa-pāl')

paraffin — la parafina (la pa-ra-fee¹-na)

parcel — el paquete (āl pa-kā¹-tā)

pardon — el perdón (āl pār-don')

to pardon — perdonar (pār-do-nar')

parents — los padres (los pa¹-drās)

park — el parque (āl par¹-kā)

to park — estacionar (ās-ta-syo-nar')

parking — aparcamiento (a-par-ka-myān¹-to);
estacionamiento (ās-ta-syo-na-myān¹-to)

parsley — el perejil (āl pā-rā-heel')

part — la parte (la par¹-tā)

particular — particular (par-tee-koo-lar')

partner — el socio (āl so¹-syo); el compañero (āl
kom-pan-yā¹-ro)

party — la fiesta (la fyās¹-ta)

to pass — pasar (pa-sar')

passage — el pasaje (āl pa-sa¹-hā)

passenger — el pasajero (āl pa-sa-hā¹-ro)

passport — el pasaporte (āl pa-sa-por¹-tā)

past — pasado (pa-sa¹-do)

pastry store — la pasterlería (la pas-tā-lā-ree¹-ya)

path — el sendero (āl sān-dā¹-ro)

patient — paciente (pa-syān¹-tā)

patio — el patio (āl pa¹-tyo)

patrol — la patrulla (la pa-troo¹-ya)

to pay — pagar (pa-gar')

pea — el chícharo (āl chee¹-cha-ro)

peace — la paz (la pas)

peaceful — tranquilo (tran-kee¹-lo)

peach — el durazno (āl doo-ras'-no)

peak — la cumbre (la koom'-brā)

peanut — el cacahuate (āl ka-ka-wa'-tā)

pear — la pera (la pā'-ra)

pearl — la perla (la pār'-la)

peasant — el campesino (āl kam-pā-see'-no)

pebble — la piedrecita (la pyā-dree'-see-ta); la guija (la gee'-ha)

peculiar — peculiar (pā-koo-lyar')

pedestrian — el peatón (āl pā-ya-ton')

pen — la pluma (la ploo'-ma)

penalty — la pena (la pā'-na); el castigo (āl kas-tee'-go)

pencil — el lápiz (āl la'-pees)

penicillin — la penicilina (la pā-nee-see-lee'-na)

penny — el centavo (āl sān-ta'-bo)

people — la gente (la hān'-tā)

pepper — la pimienta (la pee-myān'-ta)

peppermint — la menta (la mān-ta)

per — por (por)

perfect — perfecto (pār-fāk'-to)

performance — la representación (la rā-prā-sān-ta-syon')

perfume — el perfume (āl pār-foo'-mā)

perfume store — la perfumería (la pār-foo-mā-ree'-ya)

perhaps — quizás (kee-sas')

permanent — la permanente (la pār-ma-nān'-tā)

permission — el permiso (āl pār-mee'-so)

permit — el permiso (āl pār-mee'-so); la licencia (la lee-sān'-sya)

to permit — permitir (pār-mee-teer')

person — la persona (la pār-so'-na)

personal — personal (pār-so-nal')

perspiration — el sudor (āl soo-dor')

petticoat — las enaguas (las ān-a'-gwas)

pharmacist — el farmacista (āl far-ma-sees'-ta)

pharmacy — la farmacia (la far-ma'-sya)

photo store — la tienda de fotografía (la tyān'-da dā fo-to-gra-fee'-ya)

photograph — la fotografía (la fo-to-gra-fee'-ya)

photographer — el fotógrafo (āl fo-to'-gra-fo)

photography — la fotografía (la fo-to-gra-fee'-ya)

piano — el piano (āl pee-a'-no)

to pick — escoger (ās-ko-hār')

to pick up — recoger (rā-ko-hār')

pickles — los encurtidos (los ān-koor-tee'-dos)

picture — el cuadro (āl kwa'-dro)

pie — el pastel (āl pas-tāl')

piece — el pedazo (āl pā-da'-so)

pier — el muelle (āl mwā'-yā)

pig — el puerco (āl pwār'-ko)

pigeon — la paloma (la pa-lo'-ma)

pile — el montón (āl mon-ton')

pill — la píldora (la peel'-do-ra)

pillar — el pilar (āl pee-lar')

pillow — la almohada (la al-mo-a'-da)

pilot — el piloto (āl pee-lo'-to)

pin — el alfiler (āl al-fee-lār')

(safety) pin — el imperdible (āl eem-pār-dee'-blā)

pineapple — la piña (la peen'-ya)

pink — rosa (ro'-sa); rosado (ro-sa'-do)

pipe — la pipa (la pee'-pa)

pipe cleaners — las escobillas de pipa (las ās-ko-bee'-yas dā pee'-pa)

piston — el pistón (āl pees-ton')

place — el sitio (āl see'-tyo); el lugar (āl loo-gar')

to place — poner (po-nār')

plain — sencillo (sān-see'-yo)

plan — el plan (āl plan)

plane — el avión (āl a-byon')

plant — la planta (la plan'-ta)

plastic — el plástico (āl plas'-tee-ko)

plate — el plato (āl pla'-to)

platform — el andén (āl an-dān')

to play — jugar (hoo-gar')

player — el jugador (āl hoo-ga-dor')

please — por favor (por fa-bor')

to please — gustar (goos-tar')

pleasant — agradable (a-gra-daˡ-blā)
pleasure — el gusto (āl goosˡ-to)
plenty — mucho (mooˡ-cho)
plug — el enchufe (āl ān-chooˡ-fā)
plum — la ciruela (la seer-wāˡ-la)
pocket — el bolsillo (āl bol-seeˡ-yo)
pocketbook — la bolsa (la bolˡ-sa)
point — la punta (la poonˡ-ta)
points of interest — los puntos de interés (los poonˡ-tos dā een-tā-rās')
poison — el veneno (āl bā-nāˡ-no)
poisonous — venenoso (bā-nā-noˡ-so)
police — la policía (la po-lee-seeˡ-ya)
policeman — el policía (āl po-lee-seeˡ-ya)
police station — la comisaría (la ko-mee-sa-reeˡ-ya)
political — político (po-leeˡ-tee-ko)
pond — el estanque (āl ās-tanˡ-kā)
pool — la piscina (la pee-seeˡ-na)
poor — pobre (poˡ-brā)
popular — popular (po-poo-lar')
pork — el cerdo (āl sārˡ-do)
port — el puerto (āl pwārˡ-to)
port (wine) — el oporto (āl o-porˡ-to)
porter — el mozo (āl moˡ-so)
portrait — el retrato (āl rā-traˡ-to)
position — el puesto (āl pwāsˡ-to); la posición (la po-see-syon')
positive — positivo (po-see-teeˡ-bo)
possible — posible (po-seeˡ-blā)
possibly — posiblemente (po-see-blā-mānˡ-tā); tal vez (tal bās)
post office — el correo (āl ko-rrāˡ-o)
postage — el franqueo (āl fran-kāˡ-o)
postal money order — el giro postal (āl heeˡ-ro pos-tal')
postcard — la tarjeta postal (la tar-hāˡ-ta pos-tal')
postman — el cartero (āl kar-tāˡ-ro)
potable — potable (po-taˡ-blā)
potato — la papa (la paˡ-pa)

pottery — la loza (la loˡ-sa)
pound (currency) — la libra (la leeˡ-bra)
powder — el polvo (ăl polˡ-bo)
power — la fuerza (la fwărˡ-sa); el poder (ăl po-dărʹ)
powerful — poderoso (po-dā-roˡ-so)
practical — práctica (la prakˡ-tee-ka)
prayer — la oración (la o-ra-syonʹ)
precious — precioso (prā-syoˡ-so)
to prefer — preferir (prā-fā-reerʹ)
preferable — preferible (prā-fā-reeˡ-blā)
pregnant — encinta (ăn-seenˡ-ta); embarazado
   (ăm-ba-ra-saˡ-do)
premier — el primer ministro (ăl pree-mărʹ mee-neesˡ-tro)
premium — el superior (ăl soo-pā-ryorʹ); el premio (ăl
   prāˡ-myo)
preparation — la preparación (la prā-pa-ra-syonʹ)
prescription — la receta (la rā-sāˡ-ta)
present — el regalo (ăl rā-gaˡ-lo)
present — presente (prā-sănˡ-tā)
to present — presentar (prā-săn-tarʹ)
to press (iron) — planchar (plan-charʹ)
pressure — la presión (la prā-syonʹ)
pretty — bonito (bo-neeˡ-to)
to prevent — prevenir (prā-bā-neerʹ)
previous — previo (prāˡ-byo)
price — el precio (ăl prāsyˡ-o)
priest — el cura (ăl kooˡ-ra); el sacerdote (ăl sa-săr-doˡ-tā)
principal — principal (preen-see-palʹ)
print — la copia (la ko-peeˡ-ya); la estampa (la ās-tamˡ-pa)
prison — la cárcel (la karˡ-săl)
prisoner — el prisionero (ăl pree-syo-nāˡ-ro)
private — privado (pree-baˡ-do); particular
   (par-tee-koo-larʹ)
problem — el problema (ăl pro-blāˡ-ma)
to produce — producir (pro-doo-seerʹ)
production — la producción (la pro-dook-syonʹ)
professor — el profesor (ăl pro-fā-sorʹ)
program — el programa (ăl pro-graˡ-ma)

progress — el progreso (ãl pro-grãᶫ-so)
prohibited — prohibido (pro-ee-beeᶫ-do)
promenade — el paseo (ãl pa-sãᶫ-o)
promise — la promesa (la pro-mãᶫ-sa)
to promise — prometer (pro-mã-tar')
prompt — pronto (pronᶫ-to)
pronunciation — la pronunciación (la pro-noon-sya-syon')
proof — la prueba (la prwãᶫ-ba)
proper — propio (pro-peeᶫ-yo)
property — la propiedad (la pro-pee-ã-dad')
proposal — la propuesta (la pro-pwãsᶫ-ta)
proprietor — el dueño (ãl dwãnᶫ-yo)
prosperity — la prosperidad (la pros-pã-ree-dad')
to protect — proteger (pro-tã-hãr')
protection — la protección (la pro-tãk-see-on')
protestant — protestante (pro-tãs-tanᶫ-tã)
proud — orgulloso (or-goo-yoᶫ-so)
to provide — proveer (pro-bã-yãr')
province — la provincia (la pro-beenᶫ-sya)
prune — la ciruela pasa (la seer-sãᶫ-la paᶫ-sa)
public — público (poobᶫ-lee-ko)
to publish — publicar (poob-lee-kar')
to pull — jalar (ha-lar'); tirar (tee-rar')
pump — la bomba (la bomᶫ-ba)
to punish — castigar (kas-tee-gar')
pupil — el alumno (ãl a-loomᶫ-no)
to purchase — comprar (kom-prar')
pure — puro (pooᶫ-ro)
purple — morado (mo-raᶫ-do)
purpose — la intención (la een-tãn-syon')
purse — la bolsa (la bolᶫ-sa)
push — el empuje (ãl ãm-pooᶫ-hã)
to push — empujar (ãm-poo-har')
to put — poner (po-nãr')
pajamas — el pijama (ãl pee-yaᶫ-ma)
pyramid — la pirámide (la pee-raᶫ-mee-dã)
quality — la calidad (la ka-lee-dad')
quantity — la cantidad (la kan-tee-dad')

quarrel — la riña (la reen'-ya)

quarter — el cuarto (āl kwar'-to)

queen — la reina (la rāee'-na)

question — la pregunta (la prā-goon'-ta)

quick — rápido (ra'-pee-do)

quickly — pronto (pron'-to)

quiet — tranquilo (tran-kee'-lo)

quince — el membrillo (āl mām-bree'-yo)

quite — bastante (bas-tan'-tā)

rabbit — el conejo (āl ko-nā'-ho)

race — la carrera (la ka-rrā'-ra)

radio — la radio (la ra'-dyo)

radish — el rábano (āl ra'-ba-no)

railroad — el ferrocarril (āl fā-rro-ka-rreel')

rain — la lluvia (la yoo'-bya)

to rain — llover (yo-bār')

rainbow — el arco iris (āl ar'-ko ee'-rees)

raincoat — el impermeable (āl eem-pār-mā-ya'-blā)

to raise — levantar (lā-ban-tar')

raisin — la pasa (la pa'-sa)

ranch — la hacienda (la a-syān'-da); el rancho (āl ran'-cho)

rangefinder — el telémetro (āl tā-lā-mā-tro)

rapid — rápido (ra'-pee-do)

rapidly — rápidamente (ra'-pee-da-mān-tā)

rare (meat) — poco hecho (po'-co ā'-cho)

raspberry — la frambuesa (la fram-bwā'-sa)

rate — la tarifa (la ta-ree'-fa)

rather — más bien (mas byān)

rattle — el traqueteo (āl tra-kā-tā'-o)

raw — crudo (kroo'-do)

razor blades — las hojas de afeitar (las o'-has dā a-fā-tar')

to reach — alcanzar (al-kan-sar')

to read — leer (lā-yār')

ready — listo (lees'-to)

real — verdadero (bār-da-dā'-ro)

really — de veras (dā bā'-ras)

rear — de atrás (dā a-tras')

reason — la razón (la-ra-son')

reasonable — razonable (ra-so-na⸍-blā)
receipt — el recibo (āl rā-see⸍-bo)
to receive — recibir (rā-see-beer')
receiver — el auricular (āl aoo-ree-koo-lar'); el receptor (āl
  rā-sāp-tor')
recent — reciente (rā-syān⸍-tā)
reception desk — la recepción (rā-sāp-syon')
to recognize — reconocer (rā-ko-no-sār)
to recommend — recomendar (rā-ko-mān-dar')
record — el disco (āl dees⸍-ko)
to recover — recobrar (rā-ko-brar')
red — rojo (ro⸍-ho)
red snapper — el huachinango (āl wa-chee-nan⸍-go)
to reduce — reducir (rā-doo-seer')
reduction — la rebaja (la rā-ba⸍-ha); la reducción (la
  rā-dook-syon')
to refund — reembolsar (rā-ām-bol-sar')
to refuse — rehusar (rā-oo-sar')
region — la región (la rā-hyon')
to register — certificar (sār-tee-fee-kar'); registrar
  (rā-hees-trar')
to regret — lamentar (la-mān-tar'); sentir (sān-teer')
regular — regular (rā-goo-lar')
regular mail — el correo ordinario (āl ko-rrā⸍-o
  or-dee-na⸍-ree-yo)
regulation — el reglamento (āl rā-gla-mān⸍-to)
relative — pariente (pa-ryān⸍-tā)
religion — la religión (la rā-lee-hyon')
to remain — quedar (kā-dar')
to remember — recordarse (re-kor-dar⸍-sā)
to remove — quitar (kee-tar')
to renew — renovar (rā-no-bar')
to rent — alquilar (al-kee-lar')l rentar (rān-tar')
to repair — reparar (rā-pa-rar')
to repeat — repetir (rā-pā-teer')
reply — la respuesta (la rās-pwās⸍-ta)
republic — la república (la rā-poo⸍-blee-ka)
to request — pedir (pā-deer')

to rescue — salvar (sal-bar')

reservation — la reservación (la rā-sār-ba-syon')

to reserve — reservar (rā-sār-bar')

reserved — reservado (rā-sar-ba'-do)

residence — la residencia (la rā-see-dān'-sya)

restaurant — el restaurante (āl rās-taoo-ran'-tā)

restless — inquieto (een-kyā'-to)

to return — regresar (rā-grā-sar'); volver (bol-bār')

review — la revista (la rā-bees'-ta)

reward — la recompensa (la rā-kom-pān'-sa)

to rewind — robobinar (rā-bo-bee-nar')

rib — la costilla (la kos-tee'-ya)

ribbon — cinta (ceen-ta)

rice — el arroz (āl ar-rros')

rich — rico (ree'-ko)

ride — el paseo (āl pa-sā'-yo)

right (direction) — derecha (dā-rā'-cha)

(to be) right — tener razón (tā-nār' ra-son')

ring — el anillo (āl a-nee'-yo)

to ring — tocar (to-kar'); sonar (so-nnar')

ripe — maduro (ma-doo'-ro)

to rise — levantarse (lā-ban-tar'-sā); subir (soo-beer')

river — el río (āl ree'-yo)

road — la carretera (la ka-rrā-tā'-ra); el camino (āl ka-mee'-no)

roasted — asado (a-sa'-do)

to rob — robar (ro-bar')

robber — el ladrón (āl la-dron')

rock — la roca (la ro'-ka)

roll — el rollo (āl roy'-yo)

roll (bread) — el panecillo (āl pan-nā-see'-yo)

to roll — rodar (ro-dar')

(hair) rollers — los rulos (los roo'-los)

roof — el techo (āl tā'-cho)

room — el cuarto (āl kwar'-to)

to room — hospedarse (os-pā-dar'-sā)

room service — servicio de cuarto (sār-bee'-syo dā kwar'-to)

rope — la soga (la so'-ga)

rose — la rosa (la ro'-sa)

rouge — el colorete (āl ko-lo-rā'-tā)

rough — áspero (ās'-pā-ro)

round — redondo (rā-don'-do)

round trip — de ida y vuelta (dā ee'-da ee bwāl'-ta)

rowboat — la barca (la bar'-ka); la lancha (la lan'-cha)

royal — real (rā-al')

to rub — frotar (fro-tar')

rubber — el caucho (āl kaoo'-cho); el hule (āl oo'-lā)

rubbish — la basura (la ba-soo'-ra)

rude — rudo (roo'-do); grosero (gro-sā'-ro)

rug — la alfombra (la al-fom'-bra)

to ruin — arruinar (a-rroo-ee-nar')

ruins — las ruinas (las rwee'-nas)

rum — el ron (āl ron)

to run — correr (ko-rrār')

runway — la pista (la pees'-ta); la vía (la bee'-ya)

Russia — Rusia (roo'-sya)

Russian — ruso (roo'-so)

sad — triste (trees'-tā)

safe — seguro (sā-goo'-ro)

safety pin — el imperdible (āl eem-pār-dee'-blā)

to sail — zarpar (sar-par'); navegar (na-bā-gar')

sailor — el marinero (āl ma-ree-nā'-ro)

saint — el santo (āl san'-to)

salad — la ensalada (la ān-sa-la'-da)

sale — la rebaja (la rrā-ba'-ha); la venta (la bān'-ta)

salesgirl — la vendedora (la bān-dā-do'-ra)

salesman — el vendedor (āl bān-dā-dor')

salmon — el salmón (āl sal-mon')

salt — la sal (la sal)

same — mismo (mees'-mo)

(the) same (as) — lo mismo que (la mees'-ma-kā)

sample — la muestra (la mwās'-tra)

sand — la arena (la a-rā'-na)

sandals — los huaraches (los wa-ra'-chās); sandalias
  (san-da-lee-as)

sandwich — el bocadillo (āl bo-ka dee'-yo); el sandwich (āl san'-weech)

sanitary — sanitario (sa-nee-ta'-ryo)

sanitary napkins — las toallas higiénicas (las to-ay'-yas ee-hyān'-ee-kas)

satin — el raso (āl ra'-so)

satisfactory — satisfactorio (sa-tees-fak-to'-ryo)

satisfied — contento (kon-tān'-to); satisfecho (sa-tees-fā'-cho)

to satisfy — satisfacer (sa-tees-fa-sār')

Saturday — el sábado (āl sa'-ba-do)

sauce — la salsa (la sal'-sa)

saucer — el platillo (āl pla-tee'-yo)

sausage — la salchicha (la sal-chee'-cha)

to save — ahorrar (a-o-rrar')

to say — decir (dā-seer')

scale — la balanza (la ba-lan'-sa)

scar — la cicatriz (la see-ka-trees')

(to be) scared — tener miedo (tā-nār-' myā'-do)

to scar — asustar (a-soos-tar')

scarf — la bufanda (la boo-fan'-da)

scenery — el paisaje (āl pay-sa'-hā)

scent — el perfume (āl pār-foo'-mā); el olor (āl-o-lor')

schedule — el horario (āl o-ra'-ryo)

school — la escuela (la ās-kwā'-la)

science — la ciencia (la syān'-sya)

scientist — el científico (āl syān-tee'-fee-ko)

scissors — las tijeras (las tee-haā'-ras)

scooter — el escúter (āl ās-koo'-tār)

Scotland — Escocia (ās-ko'-sya)

Scottish — escocés (ās-ko-sās')

scratch — el rasguño (āl ras-toon'-yo)

sculpture — la escultura (la ās-kool-too'-ra)

sea — el mar (āl mar)

seabass — el mero (āl mā'-ro)

seagull — la gaviota (la ga-byo'-ta)

seam — la costura (la kos-too'-ra)

seaport — el puerto (āl pwār'-to)

seasick — mareado (ma-rā-a'-do)

season — la estación (la ās-ta-syon'); la temporada (la tăm-po-ra'-da)

seat — el asiento (āl a-syān'-to)

seat belt — el cinturón (āl seen-too-ron')

second — segundo (sā-goon'-do)

second class — segunda clase (sā-goon'-da kla'-sā)

secret — el secrto (āl sā-krā'-to)

secretary — el secretario (āl sā-krā-ta'-ryo)

section — la sección (la săk-syon')

sedative — el sedante (āl sā-dan'-tā); el sedativo (āl sā-da-tee'-bo)

to see — ver (bār)

to seem — parecer (pa-rā-sār')

to select — escoger (ās-ko-hār')

selection — la selección (sā-lāk-syon')

self — mismo (mees'-mo)

to sell — vender (bān-dār')

to send — mandar (man-dar')

sense — el sentido (āl sān-tee'-do)

to sense — sentir (sān-teer')

sensible — sensible (sān-see'-blā)

separate — aparte (s-par'-tā)

to separate — separar (sā-pa-rar')

September — septiembre (sāp-tyām'-brā)

series — la serie (la sā'-ryā)

serious — sério (sā'-ryo)

to serve — servir (sār-beer')

service — el servicio (āl sār-bee'-syo)

to set (the sun) — ponerse (po-nār'-sā)

to set (place) — poner (po-nār')

set meal — la comida corrida (la ko-mee'-da ko-rree'-da)

seven — siete (syā'-tā)

seventeen — diecisiete (dyās-ee-syā'-tā)

seventh — séptimo (sāp'-tee-mo)

seventy — setenta (sā-tān'-ta)

several — varios (ba'-ryos)

severe — severo (sā-bā'-ro)

114

to sew — coser (ko-sār')

shade — la sombra (la som'-bra)

shampoo — el champú (āl cham-poo')

shape — la forma (la for'-ma)

to share — repartir (rā-par-teer'); compartir (kom-par-teer')

shark — el tiburón (āl tee-boo-ron')

sharp — agudo (a-goo'-do)

shave — la afeitada (la a-fā-ee-ta'-da); la rasurada (la ra-soo'-ra-da)

to shave — afeitar (a-fā-ee-tar')

shaving cream — la crema de afeitar (la krā'-ma dā a-fa-ee-tar')

shawl — el chal (āl chal)

she — ella (ā'-ya)

sheep — el carnero (āl kar-nā'-ro); la oveja (la o-bā'-ha)

sheet — la sábana (la sa'-ba-na)

shell — la concha (la kon'-cha)

shellfish — los mariscos (los ma-rees'-kos)

shelter — el refugio (āl rā-foo'-hyo)

sherry — el jerez (āl hā-ɪās')

to shine — brillar (bree-yar')

ship — el buque (āl boo'-kā); el barco (āl bar'-ko)

to ship — enviar (ān-byar')

shipping line — la línea marítima (la lee'-nā-a ma-ree'-tee-ma)

shirt — la camisa (la ka-mee'-sa)

to shiver — tiritar (tee-ree-tar'); temblar (tām-blar')

shock — el choque (āl cho'-kā)

shoe — el zapato (āl sa-pa'-to)

shoe laces — los lazos de zapato (los la'-sos dā sa-pa'-to)

shoe repair shop — la zapatería (la sa-pa-tā-ree'-ya)

shoeshine — el lustre (āl loos'-trā); la bolada (la bo-la'-da)

shoeshine man — el limpiabotas (āl leem-pya-bo'-tas)

shoe store — la zapatería (la sa-pa-tā-ree'-ya)

to shoot — tirar (tee-rar')

shop — la tienda (la tyān'-da)

to shop — ir de compras (eer dā kom'-pras)

shopping center — el centro de compras (āl sān'-tro dā

kom'-pras)

shore — la orilla (la o-ree'-ya)

short — corto (kor'-to)

shoulder — el hombro (āl om'-bro)

show — la exhibición (la āk-see-bee-syon'); el espectáculo (āl ās-pāk-ta'-koo-lo)

to show — mostrar (mos-trar')

shower — la regadera (la rā-ga-dā'-ra); la ducha (la doo-cha)

shrimp — los camarones (los ka-ma-ro'-nās); **large shrimp** — las gambas (las gam'-bas)

shut — cerrado (sā-rra'-do)

to shut — cerrar (sā-rrar')

shutter (camera) — el obturador (āl ob-too-ra-dor')

sick — enfermo (ān-fār'-mo)

side — el lado (āl la'-do)

sidewalk — la acera (la a-sā'-ra); la banqueta (la ban-kā'-ta)

sight — la vista (la bees'-ta)

sightseeing tour — la excursión turística (la āks-koor-syon' too-rees'-tee-ka)

sign — el letrero (āl lātrā'-ro)

to sign — firmar (feer-mar')

signal — la señal (la sān-yal')

signature — la firma (la feer'-ma)

silence — el silencio (āl see-lān'-syo)

silent — silencioso (see-lān-syo'-so)

silk — la seda (la sā'-da)

silly — tonto (ton'-to)

silver — la plata (la pla'-ta)

similar — semejante (sā-mā-han'-tā); parecido (pa-rā-see'-do)

simple — sencillo (sān-see'-yo)

since — desde (dās'-dā)

to sing — cantar (kan-tar')

single — sencillo (sān-see'-yo); solo (so'-lo)

Sir — Señor (sān-yor')

sister — la harmana (la ār-ma'-na)

to sit down — sentarse (sān-tar'-sā)

six — seis (sās)

sixteen — dieciséis (dyās-ee-sās)

sixth — sexto (sāks'-to)

sixty — sesenta (sā-sān'-ta)

size — la talla (la tay'-ya); el tamaño (āl ta-man'-yo); la medida (la mā-dee'-da)

skid — patinar (pa-tee-nar'); resbalar (rās-ba-lar')

skillful — hábil (a'-beel); diestro (dyās'-tro)

skin — la piel (la pyāl)

skirt — la falda (la fal'-da)

skull — el craneo (āl kra'-nā-o)

sky — el cielo (āl syā'-lo)

sleep — el sueño (āl swān'-yo)

to sleep — dormir (dor-meer')

sleeping car — el coche-camas (āl-ko'-chā-ka'-mas)

sleeve — la manga (la man'-ga)

slice — la rebanada (la rā-ba-na'-da)

to slice — tajar (ta-har')

slides — las diapositivas (las dee-a-po-see-tee'-has)

slight — ligero (lee-hā'-ro)

slippery — resbaloso (rās-ba-lo'-so)

slope — la pendiente (la pān-dyān'-tā); la inclinación (la een-klee-na-syon')

slow — lento (lān'-to)

slowly — despacio (dās-pa'-syo)

small — pequeño (pā-kān'-yo)

smart — listo (lees'-to)

smell — el olor (o-lor')

smile — la sonrisa (la son-ree'-sa)

to smile — sonreír (son-rā-eer')

to smoke — fumar (foo-mar')

smoked — (a-oo-ma'-do)

smoker — el fumador (āl foo-ma-dor')

smooth — liso (lee'-so)

snack — el bocadillo (āl bo-ka-dee'-yo)

snail — el caracol (āl ka-ra-kol')

snapshop — la instantánea (la een-stan-tan'-ā-ya)

snow — la nieve (la nyā'-bā)

117

so — tan (tan)

soap — el jabón (āl ha-bon')

social — social (so-syal')

sock — el calcetín (āl kal-sā-teen')

soda — la soda (la so'-da)

soft — blando (blan'-do)

sold — vendido (bān-dee'-do)

sole (shoe) — la suela (la swā'-la)

sole (fish) — el lenguado (āl lān-gwa'-do)

solid — sólido (so'-lee-do)

some — algo de (al'-go dā); algunos (al-goo'-nos)

somebody — alguien (al'-gyān)

somehow — de algún modo (dā al-goon' mo'-do)

someone — alguien (al'-gyāan)

something — algo (al'-go)

sometimes — algunas veces (al-goo'-nas bā'-sās)

somewhere — en alguna parte (ān al-goo'-na par'-tā)

son — el hijo (āl ee'-ho)

song — la canción (la kan-syon')

soon — pronto (pron'-to)

sore — dolorido (do-lo-ree'-do)

sore throat — el dolor de garganta (āl do-lor' dā gar-gan'-ta)

sorrow — la pena (la pā'-na)

sorry — apenado (a-pā-na'-do)

sort — la clase (la kla'-sā)

soul — el alma (el al'-ma)

sound — el sonido (āl so nee'-do)

soup — la sopa (la so'-pa)

sour — agrio (a-gree'-yo)

south — sur (soor)

southeast — sudeste (soo-dās'-tā)

southwest — sudoeste (soo-do-ās'-tā)

souvenir — el recuerdo (āl rā-kwār'-do)

Spain — España (ās-pan'-ya)

Spanish — español (ās-pan-yol')

spark plugs — las bujías (las boo-hee'-as)

to speak — hablar (a-blar')

118

special — especial (ās-pā-syal')

special delivery — la entrega inmediata (la ān-trā'-ga een-mā-dya'-ta)

specialty — la especialidad (la ās-pā-sya-lee-dad')

speed — la prisa (la pre'-sa); la velocidad (la bā-lo-see-dad')

speed limit — la velocidad máxima (la bā-lo-see-dad' mak'-see-ma)

to spell — deletrear (dā-lā-trā-ar')

to spend — gastar (gas-tar')

spicy — picante (pee-kan'-tā)

spinach — la espinaca (la ās-pee-na'-ka)

spine — la espina (la ās-pee'-na)

to spit — escupir (ās-koo-peer')

to spoil — podrir (po-dreer')

sports — los deportes (los dā-por'-tās)

spoon — la cuchara (la koo-cha'-ra)

spot — la mancha (la man'-cha)

sprain — la torcedura (la tor-sā-doo'-ra)

to sprain — torcer (tor-sār')

spring — la primavera (la pree-ma-bā'-ra)

(bed) spring — el resorte (āl rā-sor'-tā)

squash — la calabaza (la ka-la-ba'-sa)

square — la plaza (la pla'-sa)

squid — los calamares (los ka-la-mā'-rās)

stage — el escenario (āl ā-sā-na'-ree-yo)

stain — la mancha (la man'-cha)

staircase — la escalera (la ās-ka-lā'-ra)

stairs — la escalera (la ās-ka-lā'-ra)

stamp — la estampilla (la ās-tam-pee'-ya); el timbre (āl teem'-brā)

to stand — estar de pie (ās-tar' dā-pee'-ā)

star — la estrella (al ās-trā'-ya)

starch — el almidón (āl al-mee-don')

start — el principio (āl preen-see'-pyo)

to start — empezar (ām-pā-sar')

to start up — arrancar (a-rran-kar')

starter — el arranque (āl a-rran'-kā)

119

state — el estado (āl ās-ta'-do)

stateroom — el camarote (āl ka-ma-ro'-tā)

station — la estación (la ās-ta-syon')

station platform — el andén (āl an-dān')

stationery store — la papelería (la pap-pā-lā-ree'-ya)

statue — la estatua (la ās-ta'-too-a)

to stay — quedar (kā-dar')

to stay in bed — guardar cama (gwar-dar' ka'-ma)

steak — el bistec (āl bees'-tāk)

to steal — robar (ro-bar')

steel — el acero (āl a-sā'-ro)

steep — empinado (ām-pee-na'-do)

steering wheel — el volante (āl bo-lan'-tā)

step — el paso (āl pa'-so)

stew — el guisado (āl gee-sa'-do)

steward — el camarero (āl ka-ma-rā'-ro)

stewardess — la azafata (la a-sa-fa'-ta)

stick — el palo (āl pa'-lo)

stiff — tieso (tyā'-so)

still quiet — quieto (kyā'-to)

still — todavía (to-da-bee'-ya)

sting — la picadura (la pee-ka-doo'-ra)

to sting — picar (pee-kar')

stockings — las medias (las mā'-dyas)

stolen — robado (ro-ba'-do)

stomach — el estómago (āl ās-to'-ma-go)

stomach ache — el dolor de estómago (āl do-lor' dā ās-to'-ma-go)

stone — la piedra (la pyā'-dra)

stop — la parada (la pa-ra'-da)

stop! — ¡alto! (al'-to)

to stop — parar (pa-rar')

stopover — la escala (la ās-ka'-la)

store — la tienda (la tyān'-da)

storm — la tempestad (la tām-pās-tad')

story — la historia (la ees-to'-rya); el cuento (āl kwān'-to)

straight — derecho (dā-rā'-cho)

straight ahead — derecho (dā-rā'-cho)

strange — extraño (ās-tranˡ-yo)

stranger — el extranjero (āl ās-tran-hāˡ-ro)

strap — la correa (la ko-rrāˡ-ya)

straw — la paja (la -paˡ-ha)

strawberry — la fresa (la frā-sa)

stream — el arroyo (āl a-rroyˡ-yo)

street — la calle (la kaˡ-yā)

streetcar — el tranvía (āl tran-bee-ya)

strength — la fuerza (al fwārˡ-sa)

string — la cuerda (la cwārˡ-da)

strong — fuerte (fwārˡ-tā)

structure — la estructura (la ās-trook-tooˡ-ra)

student — el estudiante (āl ās-too-dyanˡ-tā)

to study — estudiar (ās-too-dyarˡ)

stuffed — relleno (rā-yāˡ-no)

style — el estilo (āl ā-steeˡ-lo)

suburb — el suburbio (āl soo-boorˡ-byo)

to succeed — suceder (soo-sā-dārˡ); tener éxito (te-ner āk-see-to)

success — el éxito (āl ākˡ-see-to)

such — tal (tal

to suck — chupar (choo-parˡ)

suckling pig — el lechón (āl lā-chonˡ)

suddenly — de repente (dā rā-pānˡ-tā)

suede — el ante (ān anˡ-tā)

to suffer — sufrir (soo-freerˡ)

sufficient — suficiente (soo-fee-syānˡ-tā)

sugar — el azúcar (āl a-sooˡ-kar)

to suggest — sugerir (soo-hā-reerˡ)

suggestion — la sugestión (la soo-hās-tyonˡ)

suit — el traje (āl traˡ-hā)

suitcase — la maleta (la ma-lāˡ-ta)

summer — el verano (āl bā-raˡ-no)

sun — el sol (āl sol)

sunburn — la quemadura del sol (la kā-ma-dooˡ-ra dāl sol)

Sunday — el domingo (āl do-meenˡ-go)

sunglasses — las gafas del sol (las gaˡ-fas dāl sol)

sunny — asoleado (a-so-lā-aˡ-do)

sunstroke — la insolación (la een-so-la-syon')
supper — la cena (la sā'-na)
sure — seguro (sā-goo'-ro)
surface — la superficie (lā soo-pār-fee'-syā)
surprise — la sorpresa (la sor-prā'-sa)
to surprise — sorprender (sor-prān-dār')
suspect — el sospechoso (āl sos-pā-cho'-so)
to suspect — sospechar (sos-pā-char')
suspicion — la sospecha (la sos-pā'-cha)
sweater — el suétár (āl swā'-tār)
to sweep — barrer (ba-rrār')
sweet — dulce (dool'-sā)
to swell — hinchar (een-char')
to swim — nadar (na-dar')
swimming pool — la piscina (la pee-see'-na)
swollen — hinchado (een-cha'-do)
syrup — el almíbar (āl al-mee'-bar); jarabe (ha-ra'-bā)

table — la mesa (la mā'-sa)
tablecloth — el mantel (āl man-tāl')
tablet — la pastilla (la pas-tee'-ya)
tailor — el sastre (āl sas'-trā)
tailor shop — la sastrería (la sas-trā-ree'-ya)
to take — tomar (to-mar')
to take (a picture) — sacar (sa-kar')
to take long — tardar (tar-dar')
to take off — quitarse (kee-tar'-sā)
to talk — hablar (a-blar')
tall — alto (al'-to)
tank — el tanque (āl tan'-kā)
tap — la llave (la ya'-bā); el grifo (āl gree'-fo)
taste — el gusto (āl goos'-to); el sabor (āl sa-bor')
to taste diapositivas (las dee-a-po-see-tee'-bas)
taxi — el taxi (āl tak'-see)
tea — el té (āl tā)
to teach — enseñar (ān-sān-yar')

122

teacher — el maestro (ăl mạ-ā'-stro)

tear — la lágrima (la la'-gree-ma)

to tear — desgarrar (dăs-ga-rrar')

teaspoon — la cucharita (la koo-cha-ree'-ta)

teeth — los dientes (los dyăn-tăs)

telegram — el telegrama (ăl tā-lā-gra'-ma)

telephone — el teléfono (ăl tā-lā'-fo-no)

to telephone — telefonear (tā-lā-fo-nā-yar')

telephone book — le guía telefónica (la gee'-ya tā-lā-fo'-nee-ka)

telephone booth — la casilla telefónica (la ka-see'-ya tā-lā-fo'-nee-ka)

telephone operator — la telefonista (la tā-lā-fo-nees'-ta)

television — la televisión (la tā-lā-vee-sion')

to tell — decir (dā-seer')

temperature — la temperatura (la tăm-pā-ra-too'-ra)

temple — el templo (ăl tăm'-plo)

temporarily — temporalmente (tăm-po-ral-măn'-tā)

temporary — temporario (tăm-po-ra'-ryọ)

ten — diez (dyăs)

tendon — el tendón (ăl tăn-don')

tennis — el tenis (ăl tā'-nees)

tennis court — la cancha de tenis (la kan'-cha dā tā'-nees)

tent — la tienda de campaña (la tyăn'-da dā kam-pan'-ya)

tent peg — la estaquilla (la ăs-ta-kee'-ya)

tent pole — el palo de la tienda (ăl pa'-lo dā la tyăn'-da)

tenth — décimo (dā'-see-mo)

terminal — el término (ăl tăr'-mee-no)

terrace — la terraza (la tā-rra'-sa)

terrible — terrible (tā-rree'-blā)

test — la prueba (la prwā'-ba)

than — que (kā)

to thank (for) — agradecer (a-gra-dā-sār')

thank you — gracias (gra'-syas)

thankful — agredecido (a-gra-dā-see'-do)

that — que (kā)

that — ese (ā'-sā); esa (ā'-sa); eso (ā'-so)

the — el (ăl); la (la); lo (lo)

theater — el teatro (āl tā-a'-tro)

theft — el robo (āl ro'-bo)

their — su (soo)

theirs — suyo (soo'-yo)

them — los (los); las (las)

then — entonces (ān-ton'-sās)

there — allá (ay-ya'); allí (ay-yee')

(over) there — por allá (por ay-ya')

there is (are) — hay (ay)

therefore — por eso (por ā'-so)

thermometer — el termómetro (āl tār-mo'-mā-tro)

these — estos (ās'-tos); estas (ās'-tas)

they — ellos (āy'-yos); ellas (ā'-yas)

thick — grueso (grwā'-so)

thief — el ladrón (āl la-dron')

thigh — el muslo (āl moos'-lo)

thin — delgado (dāl-ga-do)

thing — la cosa (la ko'-sa)

to think — pensar (pān-sar'); creer (krā-yār')

third — tercero (tār-sā'-ro)

thirst — la sed (la sād)

to be thirsty — tener sed (tā-nār' sād)

thirteen — trece (trā'-sā)

thirty — trienta (trān'-ta)

thirty-one — treinta y uno (trān-ta-ee'-oo-no)

thirty-five — treinta y cinco (trān-ta-ee-sen'-ko)

this — este (ās'-ta); esta (ās'-ta); esto (ās'-to)

those — esos (ā'-sos); esas (ā'-sas); aquellos (a-kā'-yos)

thoroughfare — el pasaje (āl pa-sa'-hā); la vía pública (la bee'-ya poob'-lee-ka)

thousand — mil (meel)

thread — el hilo (āl ee'-lo)

three — tres (trās)

throat — la garganta (la gar-gan'-ta)

through — por (por)

through (finished) — terminado (tār-mee-na'-do)

to throw — tirar (tee-rar')

thumb — el pulgar (āl pool-gar')

124

thunder — el trueno (āl trwän-yo)

Thursday — el jueves (āl hwā'-bās)

ticket — el boleto (āl bo-lā'-to)

ticket window — la taquilla (la ta-kee'-ya); la boletería (la bo-lā-tā-ree'-ya)

tide — la marea (la ma-rā'-a)

tie — la corbata (la kor-ba'-ta)

to tie — atar (a-tar'); amarrar (a-ma-rrar')

tight — apretado (a-prā-ta'-do)

to tighten — apretar (a-prātar')

till — hasta (as'-ta)

time — el tiempo (āl tyäm-po); la hora (la o'-ra)

time (occasion) — la vez (la bās)

timetable — el horario (āl o-ra'-ryo)

tin — la lata (la la'-ta)

tip — la propina (la pro-pee'-na)

tire — la llanta (la yan'-ta)

to tire — cansar (kan-sar')

tired — cansado (kan-sa'-do)

to — para (pa'-ra); a (a)

toast — pan tostado (pan tos-ta'-do)

toasted — tostado (tos-ta'-do)

tobacco — el tabaco (āl ta-ba'-ko)

tobacco store — la tabaquería (la ta-ba-kā-ree'-ya)

today — hoy (oy)

toe — el dedo del pie (āl dā'-do dāl pee'- yā)

together — juntos (hoon'-tos)

toilet — el retrete (āl rū trā'-tā); el servicio (āl sär-bee'-syo); el baño (āl ban'-yo)

toilet paper — el papel higíenico (āl pa-pāl' ee-hyān'-ko)

token — la ficha (la fee'-cha)

tomato — el tomate (āl to-ma'-tā)

tomb — la tumba (la toom'-ba)

tomorrow — mañana (man-ya'-na)

tongue — la lengua (la län'-gwa)

tonight — esta noche (ās'-ta no'-chā)

tonsils — las amígdalas (las a-meeg'-da-lās)

too — demasiado (dā-ma-sya'-do)

too (also) — también (tam-byān')
too much — demasiado (dā-ma-sya¹-do)
tooth — el diente (āl dyān-tā)
toothache — el dolor de muelas (āl do-lor' dā mwā¹-las)
toothbrush — el cepillo de dientes (āl sā-pee¹-yo dā dyān¹-tās)
toothpaste — la pasta dentífrica (la pas¹-ta dān-tee¹-free-ka)
toothpick — el palillo (āl pa-lee¹-yo)
top — la cima (la see¹-ma)
toreador — el torero (āl to-rā¹-ro)
torn — roto (ro¹-to)
total — total (to-tal')
to touch — tocar (to-kar')
tough — duro (doo¹-ro)
tour — la excursión (la āks-koor-syon')
tourist — el turista (āl too-rees¹-ta)
tourist office — la oficina de turismo (la o-fee-see¹-na dā too-rees¹-mo)
to tow — remolcar (rā-mol-kar')
tow truck — la grua (la groo¹-a)
towards — hacia (a¹-sya)
towel — la toalla (la to-ay¹-ya)
tower — la torre (la to¹-rrā)
town — el pueblo (āl pwāb¹-lo)
toy — el juguete (āl hoo-gā¹-tā)
trade — el comercio (āl ko-mār-syo)
traffic — el tránsito (āl tran¹-see-to)
traffic circle — la glorieta (la glo-ree-ā¹-ta)
traffic light — la luz del tránsito (la loos dāl tran¹-see-to)
train — el tren (āl trān)
to transfer — trasbordar (tras-bor-dar')
to translate — traducir (trra-doo-seer')
translation — la traducción (la tra-dook-syon')
translator — el traductor (āl tra-dook-tor')
transmission — la transmisión (la trans-mee-see-on')
to travel — viajar (bya-har')
travel agency — la agencia de viajes (la a-hān¹-sya dā

bya-has')

traveler — el viajero (āl bya-hā'-ro)

traveler's check — el cheque de viajero (āl chā'-kā dā bya-hā'-ro)

tray — la bandeja (la ban-dā'-ha)

treatment — el tratamiento (āl tra-ta-myān'-to)

tree — el árbol (āl ar'-bol)

trip — el viaje (āl bya'-hā)

tropical — tropical (tro-pee-kal')

trouble — la molestia (la mo-lās-tee'-ya)

trousers — los pantalones (los pan-ta-lo'-nās)

truck — el camión (āl ka-myon')

true — verdadero (bār-da-dā'-ro)

trunk — el baúl (āl ba-ool')

truth — la verdad (la bār-dad')

to try — probar (pro-bar'); ensayar (ān-say-ar')

Tuesday — el martes (āl mar'-tās)

tuna — el atún (āl a-toon')

tunnel — el túnel (āl too'-nāl)

turkey — el guajalote (āl gwa-ha-lo'-tā); el pavo (āl pa'-bo)

turn — el viraje (āl bee-ra'-hā)

to turn — doblar (do-blar')

twelve — doce (do'-sā)

twenty — veinte (bān'-tā)

twenty-one — veintiuno (bān-tee-oo'-no)

twenty-two — veintidos (bān-tee-dos')

twice — dos veces (dos bā'-sās)

to twist — torcer (tor-sār')

two — dos (dos)

two hundred — doscientos (do-syān'-tos)

ugly — feo (fā'-yo)

umbrella — el paraguas (āl pa-ra'-gwas)

(beach) umbrella — la sombrilla (la som-bree'-ya)

uncle — el tío (āl tee'-yo)

uncomfortable — incómodo (een-ko'-mo-do)

unconscious — inconsciente (een-kon-syān'-tā)

under — debajo de (dā-ba'-ho dā)

undershirt — la camiseta (la ka-mee-sā'-ta)

127

to understand — entender (än-tän-där'); comprender (kom-prän-där')

underwater — submarino (soob-ma-ree'-no)

underwear — la ropa interior (la ro'-pa een-tä-ryor')

undress — desvestirse (däs-bäs-teer'-sä)

unequal — desigual (däs-ee-gwal')

unfair — injusto (een-hoos'-to)

unfortunate — desafortunado (däs-a-for-too-na'-do)

unhappy — infeliz (een-fä-lees')

unhealthy — malsano (mal-sa'-no); insalubre (een-sa-loo-brä)

United States — los Estados Unidos (los äs-ta'-dos oo-nee'-dos)

university — la universidad (la oo-nee-bär-see-dad')

unless — a menos que (a mä'-nos kä)

unlucky — de mala suerte (dä ma'-la swär'-ta); desafortunado (däs-a-for-too-na'-do)

to unpack — desempaquetar (däs-äm-pa-kä-tar'); desempacar (däs-äm-pa-kar')

unpleasant — desagradable (däs-a-gra-da'-blä)

unsafe — inseguro (een-sä-goo'-ro)

until — hasta (as'-ta)

untrue — falso (fal'-so)

unusual — raro (ra'-ro)

up — arriba (a-rree'-ba)

upper — superior (soo-pä-ryor')

upstairs — arriba (a-rree'-ba)

urgent — urgente (oor-hän'-tä)

us — nos (nos); nosotros (nos-o'-tros)

use — el uso (äl oo'-so)

to use — usar (oo-sar')

usual — usual (oo-soo-al')

vacant — libre (lee'-brä)

vacation — las vacaciones (las ba-ka-syo'-näs)

vaccination — la vacuna (la ba-koo'-na)

valid — válido (ba'-lee-do)

valley — el valle (äl ba'-yä)

valuable — valioso (ba-lyo'-so)

value — el valor (āl ba-lor')

valve — la válvula (la bal'-boo-la)

vanilla — la vainilla (la bay-nee'-ya)

variety — la variedad (la ba-ree-ā-dad')

vase — el florero (āl flo-rā'-ro)

veal — la ternera (la tār-nā'-ra)

vegetable — la legumbre (la lā-goom'-brā); el vegetal (āl bā-hā-tal')

vegetarian — vegetariano (bā-hā-ta-ree-ya'-no)

veil — el velo (āl bā'-lo)

vein — la vena (la bā'-na)

ventilation — la ventilación (la bān-tee-la-syon')

very — muy (mooy)

very much — mucho (moo'-cho)

vest — el chaleco (āl cha-lā'-ko)

victim — la víctima (la beek'-tee-ma)

view — la vista (la bees'-ta)

village — la aldea (la al-dā'-a)

vinegar — el vinagre (āl bee-na'-grā)

violin — el violín (āl bee-o-leen')

visa — la visa (la bee'-sa)

visit — la visita (la bee-see'-ta)

to visit — visitar (bee-see-tar')

voice — la voz (la bos)

volcano — el volcán (āl bol-kan')

voltage — el voltaje (āl bol-ta'-hā)

to vomit — vomitar (bo-mee-tar')

voyage — el viaje (āl bya'-hā)

waist — la cintura (la seen-too'-ra)

to wait — esperar (ās-pā-rar')

waiter — el camarero (āl ka-ma-rā'-ro)

waiting room — la sala de espera (la sa'-la dā ās-pā'-ra)

waitress — la camarera (la ka-ma-rā'-ra)

to wake up — despertar (dās-pār-tar')

Wales — Gales (ga'-lās)

walk — el paseo (āl pa-sā'-yo)

to walk — caminar (ka-mee-nar')

wall — la pared (la pa-rād'); el muro (āl moo'-ro)

wallet — la cartera (la kar-tā'-ra)
want — el deseo (āl dā-sā'-yo)
to want — querer (kā-rār'); desear (dā-sā-yar')
warm — caliente (kal-yān'-tā)
to warn — avisar (a-bee-sar')
warning — el aviso (āl a-bee'-so)
to wash — lavar (la-bar')
washroom — el lavabo (āl la-ba'-bo); el lavatorio (āl la-ba-to'-ryo)
washstand — el lavabo (āl la-ba'-bo)
wasp — la avispa (la a-bees'-pa)
watch — el reloj (āl rā'-loh)
watchmaker — el relojero (āl rā-lo-hā'-ro)
water — el agua (āl a'-gwa)
water jug — la garrafa (la ga-rra'-fa)
waterfall — la catarata (la ka-ta-ra'-ta)
watermelon — la sandía (la san-dee'-ya)
wave — la ola (la o'-la)
way — la vía (la bee'-ya)
we — nosotros (nos-o'-tros)
weak — débil (dā'-beel)
to wear — llevar puesto (yā-bar' pwās'-to)
weather — el tiempo (āl tyām'-po)
Wednesday — el miércoles (āl myār'-ko-lās)
week — la semana (la sā-ma'-na)
to weigh — pesar (pā-sar')
weight — el peso (āl pā'-so)
welcome — la bienvenida (la byān-bā-nee'-da)
well — bien (byān)
well (for water) — el pozo (āl po'-so)
well done (meat) — bien cocido (byān ko-see'-do)
well done (deed) — bien hecho (byān ā'-cho)
Welsh — gales (ga'-lās)
west — oeste (o-ās'-tā)
wet — mojado (mo-ha'-do)
to wet — mojar (mo-har')
what — qué (kā)
what else — qué más (kā mas)

wheel — la rueda (la rwā'-da)

when — cuándo (kwan'-do)

whenever — siempre que (syām'-prā kā)

where — dónde (don'-dā)

wherever — dondequiera (don-dā-kyā'-ra)

which — cuál (kwal)

which way — por dónde (por don'-dā)

while — mientras (myān'-tras)

a while — un rato (oon-ra'-to)

whip — el látigo (āl la'-tee-go)

whiskey — el whiskey (āl wees'-kee)

white — blanco (blan'-ko)

who — quien (kyān)

whose — de quien (dā kyān)

why — por qué (por kā)

wide — ancho (an'-cho)

width — la anchura (la an-choo'-ra); el ancho (āl an'-cho)

widow — la viuda (la byoo'-da)

widower — el viudo (āl byoo'-do)

wife — la csposa (la ās-po'-sa)

wild — salvaje (sal-ba'-hā)

willing — dispuesto (dees-pwās'-to)

to win — ganar (ga-nar')

wind — el viento (āl byān'-to)

winding — sinuoso (see-noo-o'-so)

window — la ventana (la bān-ta'-na)

(bank) window — la ventanilla (la bān-ta-nee'-ya)

windshield — el parabrisas (āl pa-ra-bree'-sas)

windshield wiper — el limpiaparabrisas (āl leem-pya-pa-ra-bree'-sas)

wine — el vino (āl bee'-no)

wing — el ala (āl a'-la)

winter — el invierno (āl een-byār'-no)

to wipe — limpiar (leem-pyar')

wise — sabio (sa'-byo)

wish — el deseo (āl dā-sā'-o)

to wish — desear (dā-sā-yar')

with — con (kon)

without — sin (seen)

woman — la mujer (la moo-hār')

wonderful — maravilloso (ma-ra-bee-yoᴸ-so)

wood — la madera (la ma-dāᴸ-ra)

woods — el bosque (āl bosᴸ-kā)

wool — la lana (la laᴸ-na)

word — la palabra (la pa-laᴸ-bra)

work — el trabajo (āl tra-baᴸ-ho)

(a) work — la obra (la oᴸ-bra)

to work — trabajar (tra-ba-har')

to work (function) — funcionar (foon-syo-nar')

world — el mundo (āl moonᴸ-do)

worried — preocupado (prā-o-koo-paᴸ-do)

to worry — preocupar (prā-o-koo-par')

worse — peor (pā-or')

worth — el valor (āl ba-lor')

to be worth — valer (ba-lār')

wound — la herida (la ā-reeᴸ-da)

to wrap — envolver (ān-bol-bār')

wrist — la muñeca (la moon-yāᴸ-ka)

wristwatch — el reloj de pulsera (āl rāᴸ-loh dā pul-sāᴸ-ra)

to write — escribir (ās-kree-beer')

writing — la escritura (la ās-kree-tooᴸ-ra)

writing paper — el papel de escribir (āl pa-pālʼ dā ās-kree-beer')

wrong — equivocado (ā-kee-bo-kaᴸ-do)

wrong number — el número equivocado (āl nooᴸ-mā-ro ā-kee-bo-kaᴸ-do)

x-ray — los rayos équis (los rayᴸ-yos āᴸ-kees)

yacht — el yate (āl yaᴸ-tā)

yard — el patio (āl paᴸ-tyo)

year — el año (āl anᴸ-yo)

yellow — amarillo (a-ma-reeᴸ-yo)

yes — sí (see)

yesterday — ayer (a-yār')

(the day before) yesterday — anteayer (an-ta-yār')

yet — todavía (to-da-beeᴸ-ya)

to yield — ceder (sā-dār')

you — usted (oo-stād'); tú (too)

young — joven (ho^L-bān)

your — su (soo)

yours — suyo (soo^L-yo)

zero — cero (sā^L-ro)

zipper — la cremallera (la krā-ma-yā^L-ra); el riqui (āl ree^L-kee)

zoo — el zoológico (āl so-o-lo^L-hee-ko)

zucchini — la calabaza (la ka-la-ba^L-sa)

SPANISH-ENGLISH GLOSSARY

a—to
a bordo—on board
abrigo—coat
abuelo—grandfather
abuela—grandmother
acento—accent
aceptar—accept
acercar—to bring closer
acompañar—to accompany
acostarse—to lie down
adiós—goodbye
adónde—where to
aeroplano—airplane
afeitarse—to shave
afuera—outside
agua—water
ahora—now
aire—air
alguien—somebody, anybody
alimento—food
almorzar—to lunch
alumno—a pupil
allí—there
amigo—a friend
andar—to walk
anoche—last night
anteojos—glasses
a pié—on foot
aquí—here
araña—spider
arreglar—to fix
arriba—up, above
arroz—rice
arte—art
asno—donkey

atizar—to poke
atrasar—to set back
autobús—bus
automóvil—automobile
avanzar—to advance
ave—bird
avenida—avenue
azúcar—sugar
azul—blue

bailar—to dance
bajo, a—low
banco—bank
bañarse—to bathe
baño—bath
barato, a—cheap
barco—ship
barrio—district
bastante—enough
batalla—battle
beber—to drink
bien—well
billete—bill
bistec—beefsteak
blandura—softness
boca—mouth
bolsillo—pocket
bondad—goodness, kindness
bonito, a—pretty
bosque—woods
botella—bottle
brazo—arm
broma—joke
bueno, a—good, kind

buenos días — good day
buenas noches — good night
buenas tardes — good afternoon
buey — ox
buho — owl

caballero — gentleman
caballo — horse
cabello — hair
cabeza — head
cada — each, every
caer — to fall
café — coffee
caja — box, case, cash box
cajero — cashier
calentar — to warm
caliente — warm, hot
calor — warmth, heat
calle — street
cama — bed
camarero — waiter, steward
cambiar — to change
caminar — to walk
camisa — shirt
campo — country, rural area
canal — channel, canal
canoa — canoe
capa — cape, cloak
capital — capital
¡caramba! — good gracious!
carbón — coal
carne — meat, flesh
carnero — sheep
caro, a — expensive, dear

carta — letter
cartera — pocket book
casa — house, home
casado, a — married
casarse — to marry, to get married
casi — almost, nearly
castillo — castle
catarro — a cold
cebolla — onion
cena — supper, dinner
céntrico, a — centrally located
centro — center
cepillar — to brush
cerca — near
cerrar — to close
cerveza — beer
charco — puddle
chofer — chauffeur
chuleta — chop, cutlet
cielo — sky, heaven
cielo raso — ceiling
cigarillo — cigarette
cima — top
cine — cinema, movies
ciudad — city
claridad — light
clasificarse — to be classified
clavel — carnation
cobrar — to collect, to charge
coger — to catch, to take
col — cabbage
coliflor — cauliflower
comedor — dining-room
comenzar — to begin
comida — food, meal, dinner
como — how, as

135

comodidad —comfort, convenience

compañía —company, society

comprar —to buy

comprobante —proof, ticket, check

comprometido, a —engaged

con —with

concierto —concert

conmigo —with me, with myself

conocer —to know

conseguir —to get, to attain

contar —to count, to tell

contestación —answer, reply

contestar —to answer

contrario, a —contrary

copo —flake

corazón —heart

corbata —tie

cordero —lamb

corneta —bugle

correcto, a —correct

corredor —corridor

corrida —run, race, bullfight

cortar —to cut

cortés —polite

cosa —thing

¿cuál? —which?

cuando —when

¿cuándo? —when?

¿cuánto? —how much?

¿cuánto tiempo? —how long?

cuarto —room

cubierto, a —covered

cuchillo —knife

cuello —neck, collar

cuenta —check, account, bill

cuerda —cord, rope, string

cuerpo —body

cuesta —it costs

cumpleaños —birthday

curso —course, direction

dar —to give

dar una vuelta —to take a walk

de —of, from

debajo de —under, beneath

deber —must, have to, to owe

decidir —to decide

decir —to say, to tell

dedo —finger, toe

dejar —to leave, to let, to allow

del —of the

delante de —before, ahead, in front of

de manera que —so as, so that, in such manner as

demasiado —too, too much

dentro de —inside of

dependiente —clerk

de prisa —fast

derecho, a —right

desagradable —unpleasant

desayunarse —to breakfast

descansar —to rest, to relax

desde —since, from

desear —to wish

deseo —wish

desgracia —misfortune, grief

desierto —desert

despedirse — to say good bye
despertador — alarm clock
despertar — to awaken
despertarse — to wake up
después — after, later
detrás — behind, after
día — day
diccionario — dictionary
diciembre — December
diez — ten
diez y nueve — nineteen
diez y ocho — eighteen
diez y seis — sixteen
diez y siete — seventeen
diferencia — difference
diferente — different
difícil — difficult
digerir — to digest
dimensión — dimension
dinero — money
dirección — direction
directamente — directly
disco — disk, record
divertido, a — funny, humorous
divertir — to amuse
divertirse — to enjoy oneself
doce — twelve
dólar — dollar
dolor — pain, ache
doméstico, a — domestic
domingo — Sunday
¿dónde? — where
dormir — to sleep
dos — two
doscientos — two hundred
dulce — sweet

durante — during
durar — to last, to wear
dureza — hardness

echar — to throw
edificio — building
ejercicio — exercise
ejército — army
el — the
él — he
eléctrico, a — electric
ella — she
ellas — they
ello — it
ellos — they
(sin) embargo — however
emperador — emperor
empezar — to begin
empleado, a — employee
empujar — to push
en — in, at, on, upon
encantado, a — delighted
encargado, a — person in charge
encender — to light, to burn
encima de — on, upon
encontrar — to find
encontrarse con — to meet with
enero — January
enfermo, a — ill
en lugar de — instead of
enojado, a — angry, cross
enojarse — to become angry, to get cross
ensalada — salad

enseguida — immediately
ensuciar — to soil
ensuciarse — to get dirty
entrar — to enter
entre — between, among, within
entonces — then
entreacto — intermission
enviar — to send
equipaje — baggage, luggage
es — it is
escaparate — shop window
escribir — to write
escuela — school
espalda — shoulder
Español, a — Spanish, Spaniard
espárrago — asparagus
especialidad — specialty
esperar — to wait (for), to hope
esposa — wife
esposo — husband
está — he is, she is, it is (position)
estación — season
estamos — we are
estampilla — stamp
estatua — statue
este, a — this
este — east
esto — this
estocada — stab
estómago — stomach
estrecho, a — narrow
estrella — star
estudiar — to study

exacto, a — exact, accurate, precise
excellente — excellent
expreso, a — expressed
expreso — express
exquisito, a — delicious
extra — extra

falda — skirt
falta — lack, fault
faltar — to fail, to lack
familia — family
favor — favor, help
(por) favor — please
febrero — February
fecha — date (of month, year)
felicitar — to congratulate
fenomenal — phenomenal
feo, a — ugly
ferrocarril — railway
fiera — wild beast
fiesta — feast
filete — steak
final — final, end
finca — real estate
flor — flower
fonógrafo — phonograph
forma — form, shape
fósforo — match
foto — snapshot
francés — French
Francia — France
frasco — flask, bottle
frase — phrase
frecuentar — to frequent, to repeat

frente — forehead
(en) frente — in front
fresa — strawberry
fresco, a — cool, fresh
frijol — bean
frío, a — cold
frito, a — fried
fruta — fruit
fuego — fire
fuera — out
función — function, performance
funcionar — to function, to perform

gafas — eye-glasses
gallina — hen
gana — desire
ganar — to gain, to win, to earn
gas — gas
gastar — to spend
gasto — expense
gato — cat
generalmente — generally
gente — people
gota — drop
gracias — thank you
gracioso, a — graceful, funny
gran — large, big, great
grande — large, big, great
gris — gray
grueso, a — thick
guante — glove
guapo, a — brave, handsome
guayaba — guava

guía — guide
guión — dash
guisante — pea
gustar — to taste, to please
gusto — taste

Habana — Havana
haber — to have (auxiliary)
habichuela — string bean
hablar — to speak, to talk
hace fresco — itis cool
hace mucho tiempo — a long time ago
hacer — to do, to make
hacer calor — to be warm, hot
hace un mes — a month ago
hacia — toward, about
hambre hunger
hamaca — hammock
hasta — till, until, up to
hasta la vista — good bye, so long
hay — there is, there are
he aquí — here is
hermana — sister
hermano — brother
hermoso, a — beautiful
hielo — ice
hiena — hyena
hija — daughter
hijo — son
historia — history, tale
histórico, a — historical
hoja — leaf, sheet (of paper)
¡hola! — hello
hombre — man

hombro — shoulder
hora — hour, time
hospedarse — to stay (at a hotel)
hoy — today

ida — departure
iglesia — church
(No) importa — it does not matter, never mind
importar — to import
impuesto — tax, duty
incluído, a — included, enclosed
incluir — to include, to enclose
indicar — to indicate, to point out
indio, a — Indian
Inglaterra — England
inglés, a — English
inmigración — immigration
innumerable — innumerable
insecto — insect
inspector — inspector
interesante — interesting
interrogación — interrogation
invierno — winter
invitación — invitation
invitado, a — guest
invitar — to invite
Italia — Italy
italiano, a — Italian
izquierdo, a — left

joven — young, young man, young woman
joya — jewel
judía verde — string bean
jueves — Thursday
julio — July
junio — June
junto — near, close, at the same time

kilo — kilogram (2.2 lbs.)
kilómetro — kilometer (⅝ of a mile)

la — the, her, it
lado — side
lago — lake
lámpara — lamp
lápiz — pencil
largo, a — long
lástima — pity
latino, a — Latin (adj.)
lavar — to wash
lavarse — to wash oneself
le — to him, to her, to it
lección — lesson
leche — milk
lechuga — lettuce
leer — to read
lejos — far
lengua — tongue, language
león — lion
les — them, to them
letra — letter
levantar — to lift, to raise

levantarse — to stand up, to get up, to rise

libertad — freedom, liberty

libertar — to free

libro — book

licor — liquor

ligeramente — lightly, slightly, quickly

limón — lemon

lindo — pretty, fine

lista — list, catalogue

listo — ready, quick, clever

lo — the, it (neuter)

lobo — wolf

localidad — place, locality, location

loma — little hill

luego — later, then next

lugar — place, spot

(en) lugar de — instead of

luna — moon

lunes — Monday

llama — flame

llamar — to call

llamarse — to be called, to be named

llave — key

llegada — arrival

llegar — to arrive, to come

llorar — to weep, to cry

llover — to rain

lluvia — rain

madera — wood

Madrid — Madrid

magnífico — magnificent

mal — evil, harm

mal — bad

maletín — valise, bag

malo, a — bad, evil

mandar — to send, to order

manecilla — hand (of a clock)

manera — manner, way, mode

mango — handle, a fruit

mano — hand

mantequilla — butter

manzana — apple, block

mañana — morning, tomorrow

mármol — marble

martes — Tuesday

marzo — March

mas — but

más — more

matador — matador, killer

matar — to kill

mayo — May

mayor — greater, greatest, larger, largest, older

media — stocking

medianoche — midnight

médico — physician

medio, a — half

medio — middle

mediodía — noon

mejor — better

melocotón — peach

menos — less, least

menú — menu

(a) menudo — often

mes — month

mesa—table
metal—metal
meter—to put in
mexicano, a—Mexican
México—Mexico
mi—my
mí—me
miedo—fear
miércoles—Wednesday
mil—thousand
milla—mile
minuto—minute
mío—mine
mirar—to look
mismo, a—same, similar
moderno—modern
mojado, a—wet
mojar—to wet
mojarse—to get wet
molestar—to disturb, to bother
molestia—annoyance, trouble
momento—moment
mono—monkey
montaña—mountain
morir—to die
mosquito—mosquito
mostrar—to show, to point out
mover—to move (something)
moverse—to move
mozo—waiter
mucho—much
muchos—(as) many
¡mucho gusto!—much pleasure!
mucho tiempo—much time, long time

muelle—dock
mujer—woman, wife
muñeca—doll
museo—museum
música—music

nacer—to be born
nada—nothing
nadie—nobody, no one
nariz—nose
necesario, a—necessary
necesitar—to need, to lack
negocio—business
negro, a—black
nevar—to snow
ni...ni—neither...nor
nieve—snow
ninguno, a—none, not any
niña—girl, child
niño—boy, child
no—no, not
noche—night
nombre—name
norte—north
norteamericano, a—North American
nos—to us, us
nosotros—we, us
novecientos—nine hundred
novia—fiancée, bride
noviembre—November
novio—bridegroom, fiancé
nube—cloud
nuestro, a—our, ours
nueve—nine
número—number, figure
nunca—never

o . . . o — either. . . or
objeto — object, thing
observar — to observe, to notice
ocasión — occasion
octavo, a — eighth
octubre — October
ocupado, a — busy, occupied
ochenta — eighty
ocho — eight
ochocientos — eight hundred
oeste — west
oficial — officer, official
oficina — office, workshop
oído — sense of hearing
oído — heard
oir — to hear
ojo — eye
oler — to smell
olor — odor, smell
olfato — sense of smell
olvidar — to forget
once — eleven
oreja — ear
órgano — organ
oro — gold
orquesta — orchestra
oso — bear
otro, a — other, another

pagar — to pay
página — page
país — country, nation
palabra — word
palacio — palace
pan — bread
pantalón — trousers

pañuelo — handkerchief
papa — potato
papas fritas — fried potatoes
papel — paper
par — equal, pair
para — for, to, in order to
parado, a — standing up
parar — to stop
paraguas — umbrella
pardo, a — brown
parecer — to appear, to seem
parecerse — to be like, to resemble
parecido, a — similar, resembling
pared — wall
París — Paris
parque — park
parte — part
pasado, a — past
pasaje — passage, ticket
pasajero — passenger, traveller
pasar — to pass, to go by, to move
pascar — to take a walk, a ride
paseo — walk, promenade, stroll
pasillo — corridor, passage
paso — step, pace
pata — leg (of an animal)
pato — duck
pavo — turkey
pavo real — peacock
peces — fish (plural)
pecho — chest
pedir — to ask for, to request
peinar — to comb
peinarse — to comb one's hair

pelota — ball
película — film
pelo — hair
péndola — pendulum
pensamiento — thought
peor — worse, worst
pequeño, a — little, small
pera — pear
percibir — to perceive
percha — peg
perder — to lose
perdonar — to forgive
perdone — pardon me
perfecto, a — perfect
perfume — perfume, odor
periódico — newspaper
permanecer — to stay, to remain
permitir — to permit, to allow
pero — but
perro — dog
persona — person
pesar — to weigh
pescado — fish (when caught)
peso — weight
pez — fish (when alive)
piano — piano
pico — beak
pié — foot
pierna — leg
pintor — painter
piña — pineapple
piso — floor, ground
pizarra — blackboard
plata — silver, money
plátano — banana
plato — dish, plate

playa — shore, beach
plaza — square, plaza
pluma — pen, feather
poco, a — little, small
poder — can, may, to be able
pollo — chicken
poner — to put
poner en hora — to set on time
ponerse — to put on
por — by, for, through
porque — because
¡por qué? — why?
portero, a — janitor
posible — possible
posición — position, status
postal — postal
postre — dessert
preceder — to precede
precio — price
precioso, a — precious, beautiful
precisar — to fix, to set
preferir — to prefer
pregunta — question
preocuparse — to worry
preparar — to prepare
prepararse — to get ready
presentar — to present, to introduce
preservar — to preserve, to keep
preservarse — to keep oneself from
primavera — spring
primero, a — first, former
principio — beginning, start, principle

producir —to produce
profesión —profession
profesor —professor
programa —program
pronto —soon, quick, fast
pronunciación —
  pronunciation
pronunciar —to pronounce
propina —tip
propósito —purpose, intention
(a) propósito —by the way
próximo —next, nearest
pueblo —town, people
puerco —pig
puerta —door
puerto —port, harbor
pues —well..., since...,
  then..., because...
pulmón —lung
punto —poiont, period
punto final —period
puro, a —pure, clear

que —that, which
¡qué? —what?
quedar —to remain, to stay
quedarse —to remain
quemar —to burn
quemarse —to burn oneself
¡qu pasa? —what is the
  matter? what happens?
¡qué tal? —how do you do?
  Hello!
querer —to want, to wish
querer a —to love
queso —cheese

¡quién? —who? whom?
quien —who, whom
quince —fifteen
quinientos, as —five hundred
quinto, a —fifth
quitar —to take away
quitarse —to take off

radiador —radiator
radio —radio
raso, a —flat, plain
rata —rat
rato —short time, a while
ratón —mouse
reanudar —to renew
recibir —to receive
recomendar —to recommend
regla —ruler, rule
reir —to laugh
reirse —to laugh
reloj —watch, clock
repaso —review, revision
reptil —reptile
reservación —reservation
reservar —to reserve, to retain
respirar —to breathe
responder —to answer, to
  reply
respuesta —answer, reply
restaurante —restaurant
retrato —picture, portrait trait
revisar —to review, to check
revista —magazine, review
rojo, a —red
romper —to break, to tear
ron —rum

rosa —rose
roto, a —broken, torn
rumba —rumba

sábado —Saturday
saber —to know
sabor —taste, flavor
sacar —to extract, to draw out
sacar fotos —to take pictures
saco —jacket, sack
sal —salt
sala —living room
salir —to go out
saltar —to jump
salud —health
salvaje —savage, wild
sangre —blood
se —oneself, himself, etc., one
   another, each other, to him,
   etc.
seco, a —dry
sed —thirst
(en) seguida —immediately
seguir —to follow, to continue
segundo, a —second
seis —six
seiscientos, as —six hundred
semana —week
sentado, a —seated, sitting
   down
sentarse —to sit down
sentido —sense
sentir —to feel
señalar —to point out
señor —sir, Mr., gentleman
señora —lady, Mrs., madam

señorita —young lady, Miss
septiembre —September
séptimo, a —seventh
ser —to be
servir —to serve, to wait on
sesenta —sixty
setecientos, as —seven
   hundred
setenta —seventy
sexto, a —sixty
sí —yes
si —if
siempre —always, ever
siesta —nap
siete —seventh
signo de admiración —
   exclamation mark
siguiente —following, next
silencio —silence
silla —chair
sin —without
sin embargo —however,
   nevertheless
sino —but, except
sírvase —please . . .
sitio —place, spot
sobre —on, upon, above
sobre —envelope
sol —sun
solamente —only
solo, a —alone
sólo —only
sombrerería —hat shop
sombrero —hat
sonido —sound
soñar —to dream
sopa —soup

soso, a — insipid, tasteless

su — his, her, its, your, their, one's

subir — to rise, to climb, to go up

sueño — sleep

suficiente — sufficient, enough

superior — superior, upper, better, finer

sur — south

suyo, a — his, hers, its, theirs, one's

tabaco — tabacco, a cigar

tacto — touch, tact

tal — such, so, as

(¡qu´tal?) — hello! how do you do?

también — also, too

tango — tango

tantos como — as many as

tarde — afternoon

(buenas) tardes — good afternoon

tarjeta — card

taxi — taxi

taza — cup

té — tea

teatro — theater

telefonear — to phone

teléfono — telephone

telefonista — telephone operator

templo — temple, church

tenedor — fork

tener — to have, to possess, to hold

tener gana de — to feel like, to wish

tener hambre — to be hungry

tener miedo — to be afraid

tener sed — to be thirsty

tercero, a — third

terminar — to finish, to end

tiempo — time, weather

tienda — shop, store

tierra — earth, land, soil, ground

tigre — tiger

tijeras — scissors

tinta — ink

tintero — inkwell

tirar — to throw, to pull

tiza — chalk

tocar — to touch

todavía — still, yet

todo, a — everything, all

todos — all

tomar — to take

toro — bull

torear — to fight bulls

trabajar — to work

traer — to bring

tráfico — trade, business, traffic

traje — dress suit

trece — thirteen

treinta — thirty

tren — train

tres — three

trescientos, as — three hundred

triste — sad, sorrowful, gloomy

trópicos — tropics

trozo — piece, part

∫**Ud.** — you

Ζ**usted** — you

Ud. mismo — yourself

último, a — last, latest, final

uno, a — one

usado, a — used, worn out

usar — to use, to wear, to accustom

usted — you

usualmente — usually

uva — grape

vaca — cow

valer — to be worthy

valor — value, price, worth, courage

varios, as — several, various

vaso — glass

verano — summer

veinte — twenty

veintidós — twenty-two

veintiuno — twenty-one

vender — to sell

ventana — window

ver — to see, to look

verdad — truth

verde — green

vestidos — dress, cloth

vestirse — to dress oneself

viajar — to travel

viaje — journey

viejo, a — old, ancient

viernes — Friday

villa — village, town

vino — wine

visible — visible

visita — visit

visitar — to visit

vista — view, panorama, sight

vivir — to live

volar — to fly

volver — to come back, to return

vuelo — flight

vuelta — return, turn

y — and

ya — already

yo — I

zanahoria — carrot

zapato — shoe

zorro — fox

SPANISH GRAMMAR

Gender

• Nouns in Spanish are either masculine or feminine.
• All articles, adjectives, pronouns must agree in number and gender with nouns to which they refer.
• Generally, nouns ending in **-o** are masculine:

el vaso — the vase
el banco — the bank
el adulto — the adult

Masculine nouns take the definite article **el**.

nouns ending in **-a** are feminine:

la caja — the box
la casa — the house
la maleta — the suitcase

Feminine nouns take the definite article **la**.

Nouns ending with other letters can be either masculine or feminine.

• the indefinite articles are **un** (before masculine nouns) and **una** (before feminine nouns)

un banco — a bank
un vaso — a vase
una caja — a box
una casa — a house

The plural forms

• Generally, for nouns ending in a vowel, add **-s** form the plural:

el vaso (the vase)	los vasos
la casa (the house)	las casas

• Otherwise, all **-es**:

el tren (the train)	los trenes
la institución (the institution)	las instituciones

Notice that the articles must be made plural also.

Possession

- To show possession, use the preposition **de**:
  (**del** is the contraction of **de** + **el**)

  > los ojos del muchaco (the boy's eyes)
  > el fin del día (the end of the day)
  > el cuarto de Roberto (Robert's room)

Adjectives

- Adjectives agree with the noun in number and gender, and generally follow the noun:

  > la cama roja (the red bed)
  > el coche rojo (the red car)

  > las camas rojas (the red beds)
  > los coches (the red cars)

- **Adjectives ending in -*e* remain unchanged whether masculine or feminine:**

  > la casa grande (the big house)
  > el coche grande (the big car)

- Possessive adjectives agree with the thing possessed, **not** the possessor:

  > mi hijo (my son)
  > mis casas (my houses)
  > su cuarto (their room)
  > sus maletas (their suitcases)

- The comparative and superlative are formed by adding **más** and **menos** before the adjective:

  > un hotel barato (a cheap hotel)
  > un hotel más barato (a cheaper hotel)
  > el hotel mas barato (the cheapest hotel)

  > un niño listo (a clever child)
  > un niño menos listo (a less clever child)
  > el ninño menos listo (the least clever child)

- When the adjective refers to a woman, the feminine form must be used:

  > Estoy enferma. (I am sick. — A woman speaking)

Está enfrema. (She is sick.)

In this book, to save space, only the masculine form of adjectives is given.

- Here are the possessive pronoun adjectives:

	singular	plural
my:	mi	mis
your:	tu	tus
his, her:	su	sus
its, your, our:	nuestro	nuestros
their, your:	su	sus

Adverbs

- Adverbs are formed by adding **-mente** to the feminine form of the adjective if there is one. Otherwise, just to the adjective:

    seguro (safe) — seguramente (safely)
    fácil (easy) — fácilmente (easily)

- Adjectives are sometimes used as adverbs.

Verbs

- In Spanish, there are three types of verbs: those with infinitives ending in **-ar, -er,** and **-ir.**

- Person is indicated by endings attached to the verb stem. There are a series of personal pronouns, but these are used mainly for emphasis.

- You, as a tourist, need not concern yourself at first with the second person forms of the verb. You use the **tu** form when you become friends with someone, and the plural **vosotros** form rarely.

    The third person form, as you can see, becomes indispensable, covering 'he,' 'she,' 'it,' and polite 'you' in the singular and 'they' and the polite 'you' in the plural.

- Here are the conjugations for regular verbs:

151

-ar verbs

ɔ́ɑr (to speak)
  hablo (I speak)   hablamos (we speak)
  hablas (you speak)   hablais (you speak)
  habla (he, she, it   hablan (they, you speak)
  speaks; you speaks)

-er verbs

vender (to sell)
  vendo (I sell)   vendemos (we sell)
  vendes (you sell)   vendies (you sell)
  vende (he, she, it   venden (they sell;
  sells; you sell)   you sell)

-ir verbs

vivir (to live)
  vivo (I live)   vivimos (we live)
  vives (you live)   vivis (you live)
  vive (he, she, it   viven (they live;
  lives; you live)   you live)

- **The negative is formed by placing *no* before the verb.**

  Es nuevo. (It's new.)
  No es nuevo. (It's not new.)

- As in all languages there are irregular verbs. These simply have to be learned. A good Spanish-English dictionary will give you the forms of the irregular verbs.

- **There are two words for the English verb to be: *ser* and *estar*.**

  Ser is used to describe a permanent condition.

  Soy americano. (I am American.)
  Soy hombre. (I am a man.)

  Estar is used to describe a temporary condition or a location.

  Estoy retrasado. (I am late.)
  Estoy en Cuba. (I am in Cuba.)

- Here are the present tense forms of these two verbs:

ser		**estar**	
soy	somos	estoy	estamos
eres	sois	estas	estaís
es	son	está	están

Word Order

- The adjective in Spanish frequently comes after the noun.

> la pelota roja (the red ball)
> es vestido azul (the blue dress)
> el río largo (the long river)

- The direct and indirect object pronouns generally precede the verb.

> Me dio el libro. (She gave me the book.)
> Me lo dio. (She gave it to me.)

- Indirect object pronouns are the same as direct object pronouns, except that **le** is used for: to him, to her, to it, and to you (polite), and **les** is used for: to them, and to you (polite, plural). The indirect object is placed first.

> Me lo vende. (He sells it to me.)

If both pronouns are third person, **se** is used as indirect object.

> Se lo vende. (He sells it to him.)

- Pronouns are often understood, and not expressed.

> ¿Habla (usted) inglés? (Do you speak English?)

- In Spanish, questions and exclamations are set off by punctuation marks at both ends of the sentence:

> ¿Que hora es? (What time is it?)
> ¿Que color hace? (How hot is it?)

Adverbs

- Adverbs are formed by adding **-mente** to the feminine form of the adjective if there is one. Otherwise, just to the adjective:

> seguro (safe) — seguramente (safely)

153

fácil (easy) — fácilmente (easily)

• Adjectives are sometimes used as adverbs.

TEMPERATURE CONVERSION

*Centigrade		*Fahrenheit
0		32
5		41
10		50
20	equals	68
30		86
40		104

To convert from *C. to *F., multiply
*C. by 1.8 and add 32.

Weight conversion

The figure in the middle stands for both kilograms and pounds, e.g., 1 kilogram = 2.205 lb. and 1 pound = 0.45 kilograms.

Kilograms (kg.)		Avoirdupois pounds
0.45	1	2.205
0.90	2	4.405
1.35	3	6.614
1.80	4	8.818
2.25	5	11.023
2.70	6	13.227
3.15	7	15.432
3.60	8	17.636
4.05	9	19.840
4.50	10	22.045
6.75	15	33.068
9.00	20	44.889
11.25	25	55.113
22.50	50	110.225
33.75	75	165.338
45.00	100	220.450

Meters and feet

The figure in the middle stands for both meters and feet, e.g., 1 meter = 3.281 ft. and 1 foot = 0.30 m.

Meters		Feet
0.30	1	3.281
0.61	2	6.563
0.91	3	9.843
1.22	4	13.124
1.52	5	16.403
1.83	6	19.686
2.13	7	22.967
2.44	8	26.248
2.74	9	29.529
3.05	10	32.810
3.35	11	36.091
3.66	12	39.372
3.96	13	42.635
4.27	14	45.934
4.57	15	49.215
4.88	16	52.496
5.18	17	55.777
5.49	18	59.058
5.79	19	62.339
6.10	20	65.620
7.62	25	82.023
15.24	50	164.046
22.86	75	246.069
30.48	100	328.092

Miles into kilometers

1 mile = 1.609 kilometers (km.)

miles	10	20	30	40	50	60	70	80	90	100
km	16	32	48	64	80	97	113	129	145	161

Kilometers into miles

1 kilometer (km.) = 0.62 miles

km	10	20	30	40	50	60	70	80	90	100	110	120	130
miles	6	12	19	25	31	37	44	50	56	62	68	75	81

Tire pressure

lb./sq. in.	kg./cm.²	lb./sq. in.	kg./cm.²
10	0.7	26	1.8
12	0.8	27	1.9
15	1.1	28	2.0
18	1.3	30	2.1
20	1.4	33	2.3
21	1.5	36	2.5
23	1.6	38	2.7
24	1.7	40	2.8

Fluid measures

liters	U.S. gal	liters	U.S. gal.
5	1.3	30	7.8
10	2.6	35	9.1
15	3.9	40	10.4
20	5.2	45	11.7
25	6.5	50	13.0

Centimeters and inches

To change centimeters into inches,
multiply by .39.
To change inches into centimeters,
multiply by 2.54.

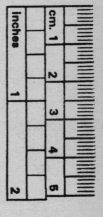

	in.	feet	yards
1 mm	0.039	0.003	0.001
1 cm	0.39	0.03	0.01
1 dm	3.94	0.32	0.10
1 yd.	39.40	3.28	1.09

	mm	cm	m
1 in.	25.4	2.54	0.025
1 ft.	304.8	30.48	0.304
1 yd.	914.4	91.44	0.914

(32 meters = 35 yards)

Clothing Sizes

Ladies

	Dresses/suits					
American	10	12	14	15	18	20
British	32	34	36	38	40	42
Continental	38	40	42	44	46	48

	Stockings						Shoes			
American	8	8½	9	9½	10	10½	6	7	8	9
British							4½	5½	6½	7½
Continental	0	1	2	3	4	5	37	39	40	41

Gentlemen

	Suits/overcoats						Shirts			
American British	36	38	40	42	44	46	15	16	17	18
Continental	46	48	50	52	54	56	38	41	43	45

	Shoes								
American British	5	6	7	8	8½	9	9½	10	11
Continental	38	39	41	42	43	43	44	44	45

SOME INTERNATIONAL ROAD SIGNS

Priority road ahead

Stop

Dangerous curve

Right Curve   **Double curve**   **Intersection**

Intersection with   **Railroad crossing**   **Railroad crossing**
secondary road   **with gates**   **without gates**

Children   **Road narrows**   **Uneven road**

Road work   **Pedestrian**   **Slippery road**
    crossing

Danger

 Traffic circle ahead

 Closed to all vehicles

 No entry

 No left turn

 No U turn

 Direction to be followed

 Speed limit

 No parking

 Customs

 No parking

 Overtaking prohibited

159

NOTES